Apostolic Succession

Apostolic Succession

An Experiment that Failed

David W. T. Brattston

Foreword by Mark E. Ryman

RESOURCE *Publications* · Eugene, Oregon

Resource Publications
An Imprint of Wipf and Stock Publishers
199 W. 8th Ave., Suite 3
Eugene, OR 97401

www.wipfandstock.com

PAPERBACK ISBN: 978-1-7252-6457-1
HARDCOVER ISBN: 978-1-7252-6458-8
EBOOK ISBN: 978-1-7252-6459-5

Manufactured in the U.S.A.   03/27/20

Except where otherwise indicated, all Bible quotations are from the Authorized (King James) version.

Except where otherwise indicated, all patristic quotations are as translated in *The Ante-Nicene Fathers: Translations of the Writings of the Fathers Down to A.D. 325* ed. Alexander Roberts and James Donaldson. American Reprint of the Edinburgh edition by A. Cleveland Coxe (Buffalo, NY: Christian Literature, 1885–96; continuously reprinted Edinburgh: T. & T. Clark; Grand Rapids, MI: Eerdmans; Peabody, MA: Hendrickson). Herein cited as "ANF." References to and quotations from Eusebius's *Ecclesiastical History* are from *Church History of Eusebius*. Translated by Arthur Cushman McGiffert (New York; Christian Literature Co.; Oxford: Parker, 1890; continuously reprinted Grand Rapids, MI: Eerdmans; Edinburgh: T & T Clark; Peabody, MA: Hendrickson). *Nicene and Post-Nicene Fathers Second Series* (*NPNF 2d*)

This book is dedicated to
the unpaid volunteers of the
Victorian Order of Nurses
Lunenburg County Site
Nova Scotia, Canada

Contents

Foreword

MY RELATIONSHIP WITH DR. David W. T. Brattston has been principally one of receiving good things from him. For almost two years, he has faithfully supplied articles for *Connections* magazine, of which I am the editor. He always delivers his articles ahead of schedule, a thing which editors find both impressive and surprising. I feel certain that I am not alone in this evaluation.

Dr. Brattston's articles delve deeply into antiquity, touching on the Church Fathers as well as the Romans and Greeks before them. He is especially interested in the Fathers, as well as early Christian epistles such as First and Second Clement, and church manuals like *The Didache*, which lie outside the canon of the New Testament. Reading his articles is often a reminder of the now faint memories of seminary. This is not to say, however, that his interests and writing are dusty. Rather, Dr. Brattston reminds us that we have a great deal in common with those who came before us. Though they laid a solid foundation for us, we still wrestle with the same themes and even many of the specifics that held the minds of our predecessors.

Therefore, it comes as no revelation that, in this volume, David Brattston tackles a matter at once ancient and modern. Before the New Testament was canonized or even available in its entirety, the early church wrestled with standards. How was the young, quickly expanding church to be governed? Who should be allowed to lead? What would church leadership look like? These were serious questions of ecclesiology without the ready answers of a complete canon of Holy Scripture. One solution was apostolic succession, and that is an option some denominations have chosen in our own day.

The theory of apostolic succession is, not unexpectedly, both old and new. We may trace its origins, as Brattston does for us, to the early church. The theory persists, sometimes through long usage, yet in newer groups or denominations, as a revived experiment in church leadership, authority, or even, perhaps, outright control. Though downplayed in some crowds, the notion of a chain of authority handed down, as believed, since the time of the apostles through the laying on of hands, remains at the ready in the background of church affairs.

Those who hold to the theory proffer apostolic succession as needful not only for legitimate bishops, but also for pastors and priests. Who may be truly ordained to serve the church? Who is able to ordain them? How is ordination rightly executed? These are serious questions with differing answers and institutional approaches that determine the most basic and central practices of the church, such as preaching and the administration of the sacraments.

David Brattston, being a retired lawyer and judge, tackles this issue with the wisdom and acumen of solid legal counsel. First, he studies the source materials and histories. Only then is he equipped to make his argument. We, the readers of *Apostolic Succession: An Experiment that Failed*, might liken ourselves to a jury. Counsel is making its case, having considered for us many stacks of books, and interviewed the sources, so that we might come to an understanding of the case before us.

With David Brattston's assistance, we will over the course of this volume, find ourselves having come to the place where we are able to make up our own minds. His title, obviously, does more than suggest his own conclusion. That is what judges do: they make decisions. This does not mean to say that the ample evidences provided in his book will not allow us to form our own conclusions. Indeed, proper evidence encourages thoughtful reflection. If we come to understand that apostolic succession is indeed a failed experiment, we will be better equipped to realize why this is so.

A standard argument in the theory is whether apostolic succession relates to the authority of the apostles handed down to others, or to the doctrines they handed down: the teachings of the Scriptures. Is the real authority that of the Word, rather than being essentially ecclesiastical in nature? Counsel provides both the evidence and the arguments needful for our consideration. In doing so, one may discover a difference between orthodoxy and orthopraxy: correct doctrine and right practice. In the pages that follow, we may decide that one does not necessarily follow the other, and that the ostensible orthopraxy of apostolic succession may actually stifle orthodoxy.

The issue is important, even vital, to a proper understanding of the Christian past, as well as to providing us with the necessary tools for finding our way through the present. Dr. David W. T. Brattston has provided the means in the book you are holding, so that listening with him to the past, we may find the present clearer, and the future, perhaps, more promising.

Rev. Mark E. Ryman
Production Editor
Sola Publishing
Graham, North Carolina

1

Meaning of "Apostolic Succession"

APOSTOLIC SUCCESSION IS THE doctrine or theory that the legitimate ministry of the Christian Church comes through a continu-
ous succession of incumbent bishops ordaining new clergymen,
such as a new bishop, by laying their hands on him. Such ordination gives him key authority over public worship, rulership of the
church, and ordaining presbyters, deacons, and other bishops. It is
essential that the ordaining bishops themselves have been ordained
by similar bishops who had been ordained by similar bishops in
an unbroken line which stretches back to the apostles. According
to its adherents since the Reformation, such apostolic succession
is indispensable for the sacraments of an individual clergyman to
be valid and in conformity with church law, guarantees doctrinal
orthodoxy and correctness in public worship, and gives authority
to the ordain presbyters (priests), deacons, and other bishops. In
our time, ordination in the apostolic succession confers the right
to govern the church in the geographic area assigned to a bishop,
usually a diocese consisting of several congregations. He is the
ultimate authority within the area allotted to him. Apostolic succession is held and practiced as vital to church life by the Roman
Catholic church, the Eastern Orthodox, the Oriental Orthodox
(derisively called "monophysites"), the Assyrian Church of the
East ("Nestorians"), Anglicans/Episcopalians, and some other

denominations with an episcopal, hierarchical, polity. Some denominations which believe themselves to be in the apostolic succession do not recognize the status or lineages of some other families of denominations which claim it, but in recent decades some families of denominations have begun recognizing the apostolic succession of others. Clergy that convert from one family to another are often ordained again, as are converts from Protestant denominations that do not believe in it, which implies that the original denomination lacked an essential facet of church life.

Apostolic succession is not in the Bible, nor should we expect to see it there. It is a program for how Christians should cope with issues that did not arise until after the New Testament was completed. It is proposed as a method for ascertaining which among several doctrines is correct and for disseminating correct ones. As long as there was recourse to living apostles who had been trained by Jesus personally, there was no need to look elsewhere. Apostolic succession is seen as the best and only legitimate replacement for functioning without such personal contact, now for almost two thousand years. This succession is alleged to give legitimacy to the church and provide God's authority to its administrative and sacramental officers.

Apostolic succession is different from apostolic tradition. The apostolic succession is a line of people throughout history dating back to the time of the apostles. The apostolic tradition is the substance of the teachings of the original church, as evidenced to a particular date. The terminal date has long been in dispute. The content of the apostolic tradition is straightforward enough to ascertain, if a person is prepared to do enough reading of the extant early sources, all but one of which have been translated into English or French. Many appear on the internet. In fact, they provide us with an advantage most early Christians did not possess, for the full text of the New Testament and thoughts of other Christian writers were seldom available at the time of the formulation of the theory of apostolic succession.

During the period under discussion in this book, a bishop was a congregational official. Together with the presbyters (elders) and deacons, he led the local church. A bishop was not distinct from the other elders in the New Testament period nor in western Europe prior to the middle of the second century. Monepiscopacy (a single rather than several bishops in a local congregation) began in the Middle East in the late first or early second century and slowly spread westward, reaching the City of Rome by the middle of the second. Although a man could be bishop or pastor of two congregations simultaneously, the institution of one bishop governing a number of congregations in a single diocese did not begin until the middle of the third. Since the Reformation, it has been debated whether the true modern equivalent of a Biblical bishop is a pastor of a congregation or small number of self-governing congregations on the one hand (presbyterian polity, congregational polity) or is the leader of many congregations which depend on him as chief legislator (diocesan, episcopal polity), such as Anglican and Orthodox, with Roman Catholicism as a variant of episcopacy whose ultimate leader is the pope of Rome as bishop of bishops. Apostolic succession is held to especially by denominations with episcopal polities, while those with presbyterial and congregational structure deny that it has any value or simply did not exist in the early Christian centuries. Monopoly over doctrinal orthodoxy has come to include the sole authority to interpret the Bible and early sources correctly, which leads to the episcopally-ordained bishops having final word on the appropriate form of church government and teaching as a matter of doctrine.

Since the Middle Ages, the following types of exclusive ecclesiastical powers are alleged to be transmitted to clerics in the apostolic succession as part and parcel of their office: to govern the church spiritually and materially, to validate sacraments except baptism, to decide and teach points of doctrine, to ordain presbyters and deacons, to collect money, and to transmit the succession to future bishops.

Some Anglican candidates for the ordained ministry doubt whether certain of their bishops possess true lines of succession from the apostles, being descended from a pedigree when valid ordination rites were temporarily suspended in the Church of

England. Such candidates are assiduous in seeking ordination from the successors of bishops who held the proper pedigree who entered the Anglican line after the Reformation. This demonstrates the importance and faith of some people who believe sacraments, doctrinal orthodoxy, and ecclesiastical governance to be invalid or illegitimate outside an uninterrupted lineage from the apostles.

2

Need to Study the Origins

MOST REFORM AND RENEWAL movements in Christianity assert that their aim and teachings are a return to the original, pristine, Christian faith.[1] Longstanding traditional ones, especially denominations with an episcopal polity, usually assert that they have maintained it all along. Study of the early sources is an indispensable guide to what this faith was like, and provide a gauge to see how well they accomplish their purpose.

To avoid reading into the Christian past, or any past, only what we want to see there, we must obtain knowledge of the real past, based on the best evidence procurable of what that past really was. Drawing from sources originating centuries after the events can yield errors and misconceptions. The best possible evidence comes from people who were personally acquainted with the characters, thought, and events of the era, or at least not many hands removed from them. Thus, consulting the earliest nonbiblical sources about New Testament and other pristine Christianity is superior to consulting sources that came much later in time—many over a millennium and a half—in which there was plenty of opportunity for misconceptions, deceptions, and other errors to

---

1. Daniel H. Williams, *Retrieving the Tradition*, 26, 218. He is professor of patristics and historical theology at the Department of Religion, Baylor University.

creep in and distort their perceptions and knowledge or render them wildly incorrect.

The probability is vanishingly remote that even the most dedicated and protracted study of the Scriptures in the sixteenth century or later would uncover an important spiritual truth unknown to early Christians. Christianity has never been a mere collection of writings that can be interpreted by one person as accurately as by another regardless of time or place. The Christian faith has always been a living community or group of communities in which the gospel is shared and transmitted. One Christian interacts with others; older members tell younger members; unwritten memories are recorded in writing by a later generation; and each person directly or indirectly interacts with other Christians from whom they are not isolated by geography. Everyone dies sometime and recollections grow dim, thus gradually weakening the recollections of earlier times and practices. The full meaning and milieu of the Christian message (including the New Testament) gradually fades over the generations. Thus, we need the witness of as many as possible of the early heirs of the gospel, i.e., believers who had been personally acquainted with the apostles or their early disciples who had inherited much fresher memories of Christ and His teaching, in preference to those of later decades or centuries. The present book therefore consults all truly ancient Christian writings, letting all available voices be heard, not just those judged orthodox by their own or a later age. Such inclusiveness (1) avoids applying suppositions as to what is true or authentic Christianity by the criteria of a later time or of a rival denomination within its own time, (2) provides a fuller view of the subject-matter, (3) avoids straightjacketing the literature by my own—or my age's—unwitting assumptions or presuppositions, and (4) gives the consensus of the whole of the Christianity of its day instead of a single denomination or author.

The written word has no effect until read and understood by human beings, who vary in their ability to interpret and understand. The concept of rejecting guidance from outside the Scriptures is really guidance by an interpretation of Scripture, usually an interpretation which dates back no further than five hundred years at most. Bible passages do not select themselves nor do they arrange themselves of their own accord to produce the most correct exegesis.[2] In contrast, where the early Christian authors agree among themselves, it must be deduced that their interpretations were made within a milieu received from the apostles not many years earlier. They too present only an interpretation, but it is a better interpretation than those formulated since the sixteenth century because it was made closer in time, life, culture, and way of thinking to the authors of the New Testament, with whom some of them were personally acquainted. It is also more neutral than some diocesan bishops' self-serving interpretation that Scripture authorizes only an episcopal polity for the church.

Christians who seek to reform or "restore" the original faith will benefit from study of the antiquities because they give possible scenarios of what might happen to their movement after they leave the scene, when they see what happened after the deaths of the apostles. The rise and fall of Christian movements since the Reformation demonstrate that the mere lawful and recognized transfer of office from a churchman to his successors does not necessarily convey all the qualities and abilities of the founder of the movement. Often a charismatic individual has established a denomination or movement which becomes very popular and influential. After he leaves office, even his handpicked successor does not measure up to his skills in teaching, charming people, preaching, Bible analysis and creativity, gifts for church administration, or instilling enthusiasm. Although possessing all the founder was able to give, successors do not inherit all his attributes, and the movement later becomes a mere shell. Without the founder's gifts and competence, the old charisma and power are gone. Often later followers see schism as a means of regaining the old spirit and authority. A good example is the Worldwide Church of God, founded less than a century ago by the charismatic Herbert W. Armstrong. In addition to "restoring many important doctrines to the church,"

2. The ideas in this sentence are not original to me. They stuck in my mind some years ago but I have not been able to find their source again.

he criticized the established denominations because they were divided and fragmented, and proposed that Christendom should be united again, under his banner. Within a few years of his death, it lost about ninety percent of its followers and finances, and divided into over three hundred new denominations, each criticizing the other for false teaching and contributing to division in Christianity. Clearly, not all his gifts, abilities, and attributes could be inherited. Thus, the powers given to the apostles did not necessarily descend to their successors, by mere virtue of apostolic succession. To see which ones were in fact passed on, we need to examine Christian literature of the period following the deaths of the apostles.

More relevant to the present book was the Apostle Simon Peter. Peter personally possessed the ability to heal, raise the dead, and confer other supernatural gifts of the Holy Spirit (Acts 3:2–8, Acts 5:12, 15–16, Acts 8:6–7, 16–17, Acts 9:33–34, Acts 9:37–38), but he did not pass them on to anyone else, as shown in the cases of Philip the Evangelist in Acts 8 and the Christians at Lydda in Acts 9:38, although we know these powers survived into the early centuries.[3] Acts 3:6 portrays Peter as penniless as a result of following Christ, but his alleged successors are not. He possessed the power to kill mendacious donors supernaturally (Acts 5:1–10), which modern bishops do not share. Certainly, whoever may have succeeded him as the bishop of Antioch or Rome in Catholic reckoning did not inherit Peter's wife! Thus, a line of succession in office does not necessarily confer all the abilities and authority of the apostles.

---

3. *Didache* 11.7–8, 11.12, 13.1–7; Quadratus, *Apology*; Justin Martyr, *Dialogue with Trypho* 30; Irenaeus, *Against Heresies* 2, 31.2, 2.32.4, Theophilus of Antioch, *To Autolycus* 2.8, Origen, *Against Celsus* 1.6, 1.46, 1.67, 7.8, 7.67, Origen, *Commentary on the Song of Songs* Prologue, ch. 4, Origen, *Homilies on Isaiah* 6, Origen, *Homilies on Exodus* 13.2, Tertullian,. *Soul's Testimony* 3, Tertullian, *To Scapula* 2, Tertullian, *Against Marcion* 5.8; *Martyrdom of Pionius* 13.6; Cyprian, *Letter* 69.15; Firmilian, *Letter* 75.10 in the collection of Cyprian; Arnobius, *Against the Heathen* 46; *Martyrdom of Marian and James* 12.7.

3

Earliest Arguments for Apostolic Succession

A—Succession in the New Testament Period

ADVOCATES OF THE NECESSITY of apostolic succession state that it is rooted in Christian antiquity, as witnessed in the Acts of the Apostles, the Pastoral Epistles, the *First Epistle of Clement*, the writings of Bishop Irenaeus of Lyons late in the second century, of Tertullian around AD 200, and of Christian writers of like vintage. The following chapter outlines them.

According to Acts 13:1–3, Paul and companions were commissioned as missionaries by a group of prophets and teachers within the church at Antioch, not the whole church or a bishop or another apostle, with prayer, fasting, and laying on hands. Acts 14:23 records that Paul and Barnabas in turn ordained elders with prayer and fasting in every church of a missionary field, but does not comment on the purpose or the powers granted to these new church officers. From Acts 15 it appears that elders filled some sort of important deliberative role.

In 1 Timothy 1:3, 4:6, and 11, and 2 Timothy 2:2 and 2:14, the Apostle Paul is depicted as instructing his younger colleague and disciple Timothy to perform tasks elsewhere those of an apostle, which witnesses the link between the apostles and later Christians they knew personally. The earliest reference seen as supporting the doctrine of apostolic succession is 2 Timothy 2:2, which relates that Paul conferred all or some of the apostolic capacities on a Christian of a younger generation, especially the teaching office: "And the things that thou hast heard of me among many witnesses, the same commit thou to faithful men, who shall be able to teach others also." Note the reference to a third generation, who were to carry on this teaching into another century. This does not specify bishops or elders of a local congregation, which were interchangeable designations in this time period, and relates to teaching and doctrine, not church government or discipline, or the validity of sacraments. Under the theory, a line of ordinations must begin with an apostle, but from 1 Timothy 4:14 and 2 Timothy 1:6 it is unclear whether Timothy was ordained by a college of presbyters or by the Apostle Paul alone.

The next reference is in the Epistle to Titus. According to the King James Version, Paul purportedly commanded: "For this cause left I thee in Crete, that thou shouldest set in order the things that are wanting, and ordain elders in every city, as I had appointed thee:" (Tit 1:5). The Douay-Rheims 1899 American Edition has "shouldest ordain priests in every city." The NRSV and NASB translate as "appoint elders." The original verb is *kathistemi*. It has a wide range of translations in English New Testaments, but the only two uses in the context of causing someone to become a religious officeholder are the Old Testament high priest in Hebrews 5:1, 7:28, 8:3, and the selection and installation of the seven "deacons" in Act 6:3. In the latter case, the apostles left the nomination of candidates to "the whole multitude," i.e. the Christian congregation. Titus was commanded to appoint presbyters, not necessarily bishops, and not necessarily without prior approval by the laypeople to be affected.

B—*First Clement*: Mid-or Late-first Century, While Some Apostles Were Still Alive

In the middle or late first century, the church in the City of Rome sent a letter to that at Corinth because malcontents in the latter had deposed clergy ordained by the apostles and/or officeholders who were their designated successors. The letter advocated that those in the succession from the apostles should be restored. *First Clement* 42 wrote of the apostles: "And thus preaching through countries and cities, they appointed the first-fruits [of their labours], having first proved them by the Spirit, to be bishops and deacons of those who should afterwards believe,"[1] and at Chapter 44:

> Our apostles also knew, through our Lord Jesus Christ, and there would be strife on account of the office of the episcopate. For this reason, therefore, inasmuch as they had obtained a perfect fore-knowledge of this, they appointed those [ministers] already mentioned, and afterwards gave instructions, that when these should fall asleep, other approved men should succeed them in their ministry. We are of opinion, therefore, that those appointed by them, or afterwards by other eminent men, with the consent of the whole church, and who have blamelessly served the flock of Christ in a humble, peaceable, and disinterested spirit, and have for a long time possessed the good opinion of all, cannot be justly dismissed from the ministry.

Note, for later discussion, the phrase "with the consent of the whole Church," which indicates that the laity of the particular church participated in the choice and installation of their bishop.

C—Hegesippus: Mid-second Century

In the middle of the second century, a converted Jew named Hege-sippus travelled from the Levant as far as Rome to ascertain which

---

1. The Apostle Paul wrote in 1 Corinthians 16:15–16 of an entire "house-hold" as being in this category.

local congregations had kept the pure doctrine of the apostles. His conclusion was that it had been maintained in the teaching handed down through the succession of bishops, but gave way to heresies in the third generation in some congregations. To this end, he drafted lists of bishops for a few or each locality, and concluded that Christianity had everywhere remained doctrinally pristine until the second or third bishop after the apostles.

D—Irenaeus: AD 180s

Bishop Irenaeus of Lyons was a member of the denomination of Christians known as the "catholics" or "Great Church," and the first exponent of Christian succession to write at length. He had received his early Christian formation at Smyrna in Anatolia, largely under Polycarp, who had been installed bishop of the church there by the apostles themselves. At the time Irenaeus wrote *Against Heresies,* his field of ministry was in southern France, in the course of which he was in much contact with the bishops of Rome. His *Against Heresies* was a refutation of various denominations of Gnostic Christianity and their interpretations of the Scriptures. Much of the Gnostics' energies were applied to deciphering and explaining the Scriptures in ways that would promote their exotic religious and cosmological theories. In arguing against them, Irenaeus labored under the impediments that any Bible passage can be interpreted more than one way and the Gnostics could argue that it was the catholic interpretation that was flawed by faulty hermeneutics rather than their own. To overcome this hurdle, he raised eight arguments which were not available to them. In defending a specific tenet of theology, Irenaeus contended that proof for it could be deduced from (1) the universality of human belief, even among pagans, (2) its acceptance from time immemorial, "from the tradition of the first-formed man," (3) the prophets reminding men of it, (4) "The Universal Church, moreover, through the whole world, has received this tradition from the apostles."[2]

---

2. Irenaeus, *Against Heresies* 2.9.1 (ANF 1:369).

(5) the orthodox/catholic church possessed a tradition of beliefs and practices or of hermeneutics which had been handed down unbroken and unimpaired from the apostles, (6) orthodox Christian communities were found throughout the known world while heresies tended to be local in extent, (7) adherents of the catholic interpretation were in unity with each other all over the known world, in contrast to local variations among the heresies, and (8) the guardians of this tradition (presbyter-bishops in the catholic of Great Church), who were the successors of the apostles, accepted the catholic interpretation over the Gnostics'. Irenaeus said that it was these eight factors rather than any pretended superiority in the method of Bible interpretation that ensured the correct exegesis of the Scripture.

Irenaeus contended that a diligent investigator can see the truth and "contemplate clearly the tradition of the apostles throughout the whole world" by consulting bishops who had been ordained by bishops who had themselves been ordained by bishops, etc., in lines stretching back to ordinations by apostles. He said that such lines of succession could be traced down to "our own times," i.e. the A.D 180s:

> It is within the power of all, therefore, in every Church, who may wish to see the truth, to contemplate clearly the tradition of the apostles manifested throughout the whole world; and we are in a position to reckon up those who were by the apostles instituted bishops in the Churches, and [to demonstrate] the succession of these men to our own times; those who neither taught nor knew of anything like what these [heretics] rave about. For if the apostles had known hidden mysteries, which they were in the habit of imparting to the perfect apart and privily from the rest, they would have delivered them especially to those to whom they were also committing the Churches themselves. For they were desirous that these men should be very perfect and blameless in all things, whom also they were leaving behind as their successors, delivering up their own place of government to these men; which men, if they discharged their functions

honestly, would be a great boon [to the Church], but if they should fall away, the direst calamity.[3]

Irenaeus *Against Heresies* 4.26.2:

> Wherefore it is incumbent to obey the presbyters who are in the Church,—those who, as I have shown, possess the succession from the apostles; those who, together with the succession of the episcopate, have received the certain gift of truth, according to the good pleasure of the Father. But [it is also incumbent] to hold in suspicion others who depart from the primitive succession, and assemble themselves together in any place whatsoever, [looking upon them] either as heretics of perverse minds, or as schismatics puffed up and self-pleasing, or again as hypocrites, acting thus for the sake of lucre and vainglory.[4]

Against Heresies 3.4.1:

> Suppose there arise a dispute relative to some important question among us, should we not have recourse to the most ancient Churches with which the apostles held constant intercourse, and learn from them what is certain and clear in regard to the present question? For how should it be if the apostles themselves had not left us writings? Would it not be necessary, [in that case,] to follow the course of the tradition which they handed down to those to whom they did commit the Churches?[5]

Against Heresies 4.26.4: "adhere to those who, as I have already observed, do hold the doctrine of the apostles, and who, together with the order of priesthood (*presbyterii ordine*), display sound speech and blameless conduct for the confirmation and correction of others."[6]

Against Heresies 4.32.1: "And then shall every word also seem consistent to him, if he for his part diligently read the Scriptures

3. Irenaeus, *Against Heresies* 3.3.1 (ANF 1:415).
4. ANF 1:497.
5. ANF 1:417.
6. ANF 1:497.

in company with those who are presbyters in the Church, among whom is the apostolic doctrine, as I have pointed out."[7]

Against Heresies 4.26.5:

> Where, therefore, the gifts of the Lord have been placed, there it behoves us to learn the truth, [namely,] from those who possess that succession of the Church which is from the apostles, and among whom exists that which is sound and blameless in conduct, as well as that which is unadulterated and incorrupt in speech. For these also preserve this faith of ours in one God who created all things; and they increase that love [which we have] for the Son of God, who accomplished such marvellous dispensations for our sake: and they expound the Scriptures to us without danger, neither blaspheming God, nor dishonouring the patriarchs, nor despising the prophets.[8]

Against Heresies 4.33.8:

> True knowledge is [that which consists in] the doctrine of the apostles, and the ancient constitution of the Church throughout all the world, and the distinctive manifestation of the body of Christ according to the successions of the bishops, by which they have handed down that Church which exists in every place, and has come even unto us, being guarded and preserved, without any forging of Scriptures, by a very complete system of doctrine.[9]

Against Heresies 5.20.1:

> Now all these [heretics] are of much later date than the bishops to whom the apostles committed the Churches; which fact I have in the third book taken all pains to demonstrate. It follows, then, as a matter of course, that these heretics aforementioned, since they are blind to the truth, and deviate from the [right] way, will walk in various roads; and therefore the footsteps of their doctrine

---

7. ANF 1:506.
8. ANF 1:498.
9. ANF 1:508.

are scattered here and there without agreement or connection. But the path of those belonging to the Church circumscribes the whole world, as possessing the sure tradition from the apostles, and gives unto us to see that the faith of all is one and the same.[10]

Irenaeus asserted that all these bishops accepted the catholic faith (the faith that had been transmitted by the succession in the Great Church and tradition) and were contemporary guardians of the apostolic tradition.[11]

For Irenaeus, purity of the Christian faith was so important that God had instituted a special office of guardians to protect and impart it. Advocates of apostolic succession call them "bishops." By way of illustration, *Against Heresies* 3.3.3 contains succession-lists or pedigrees of ordinations to the clergy at Smyrna and Rome, down to the late second century, including information that Peter and Paul ordained Linus as the first Roman bishop, who was succeeded in order by Anacletus, Clement, Evaristus, Alexander, Sixtus, Telephorus, Hyginus, Pius, Anicetus, Soter, and Eleutherius.[12]

On a more personal level than *Against Heresies*, Irenaeus wrote a letter to a Christian named Florinus to refute the belief that God is the author of evil. In criticizing Florinus' doctrines, Irenaeus stated that they were "not of sound judgment," "disagree with the Church," "not even the heretics outside of the Church, have ever dared to publish" them, and "the presbyters who were before us, and who were companions of the apostles, did not deliver [them] to thee."[13] To reinforce the last mentioned, he reminisced about Polycarp, whom both Irenaeus and Florinus had known in their youth. Here Irenaeus used post-Biblical Christian teaching from a bishop in the apostolic line, or student of an apostle, as an authority in a dispute with a dissident Christian who had first-hand knowledge of the extra-biblical sources Irenaeus cited and

10. ANF 1:547–48.

11. Irenaeus, *Against Heresies* 3.3.1.

12. Irenaeus, *Against Heresies*, 3.3.3.

13. Irenaeus, *Letter to Florinus*. In Eusebius *History of the Church* 5.20.4 trans. Arthur Cushman McGiffert NPNF 2d 1:238.

thus would have been able to refute Irenaeus's argument if the tradition supported Florinus's own position.

E—Clement of Alexandria: AD 190s

Another Clement, Clement of Alexandria in Egypt, wrote of what might be construed as a succession. As dean or principal of the leading institution of Christian higher education of the day, he flourished a decade after Irenaeus and a decade before Tertullian. Writing of Christians of the generation older than his own who had taught him the Christian faith, Clement recorded that one such teacher was in Greece proper, another in Ionia, another in Syria, others in Egypt, and others in "the East." One was born in Assyria "and the other a Hebrew in Palestine." Clement praised them because

> they preserving the tradition of the blessed doctrine de-
> rived directly from the holy apostles, Peter, James, John,
> and Paul, the sons receiving it from the father (but few
> were like the fathers), came by God's will to us also to
> deposit those ancestral and apostolic seeds. And well I
> know that they will exult; I do not mean delighted with
> this tribute, but solely on account of the preservation
> of the truth, according as they delivered it. For such a
> sketch as this, will, I think, be agreeable to a soul desirous
> of preserving from escape the blessed tradition.[14]

Clement of Alexandria did not identify teachers as specifically bishops, or even clergy. In this passage, the succession relates to the *doctrine* of the apostles, not their authority to govern
Christians' lives or to set rules. What was important to him was the
apostolic tradition, a body of knowledge. Although he mentioned
bishops, presbyters, and deacons at *Stromata* 6.13, he did not dis-
tinguish bishops from presbyters. Nowhere did he allude to how
the church of the AD 190s was organized or administered or how
they obtained their offices.

---

14. Clement of Alexandria, *Stromata* 1.1 (ANF 2:301).

Indeed, Clement did not confine apostolic succession to the clergy:

> Those, then, also now, who have exercised themselves in the Lord's commandments, and lived perfectly and gnostically according to the Gospel, may be enrolled in the chosen body of the apostles. Such an one is in reality a presbyter of the Church, and a true minister (deacon) of the will of God, if he do and teach what is the Lord's; not as being ordained by men, nor regarded righteous because a presbyter, but enrolled in the presbyterate because righteous. And although here upon earth he be not honoured with the chief seat, he will sit down on the four-and-twenty thrones, judging the people, as John says in the Apocalypse.[15]

F—Tertullian: AD 198 to about 220

Tertullian is of double value to the inquirer into Christian antiquities soon after the apostles. He wrote from both inside the catholic or Great Church, and later from a breakoff from it, the Montanists, who believed the Holy Spirit did not descend on the Twelve Apostles, but on the Montanist prophets in the middle of the second century. They were rigorists who condemned mainline or orthodox Christianity for its laxity in lifestyle and seeming lack of the Holy Spirit. Tertullian may be of triple value, because in his Montanist writings he quoted and described the doctrines and practices of the Great church in order to refute them.

Prior to his conversion to Christianity and becoming a clergyman, he had been a prominent lawyer in the City of Rome. Called "the Father of Latin Christian Literature," he wrote more on Christian topics in the Latin language before Augustine two centuries later, when the secular government favored Christian writing.

In his early, catholic, writing, Tertullian stated that the congregations founded by apostles had received their faith in two

---

15. Clement of Alexandria, *Stromata* 6.13 (ANF 2:504).

ways: oral preaching and written letters.[16] He attributed a number of important features of church life solely to the unimpaired continuation of the apostolic tradition through the apostolic succession: the apostolicity, unity, communion in peace, fraternal spirit, and practice of mutual hospitality among catholic congregations.[17] In order to refute the proposition put forward by non-catholics that at one time or another in the first two centuries the Great Church had apostatized from the original gospel and remained apostate in Tertullian's day, he pointed to the accepted fact that its catholic congregations throughout the known world all taught the same things, and from this he argued that the sameness was proof that catholic churches were preaching and teaching the original and uncorrupted gospel. If, said Tertullian, distinctively catholic doctrine were the result of congregations straying from the original Christian message by creating something new, the various churches would necessarily have strayed haphazardly and randomly and have produced different beliefs and practices: "When, however, that which is deposited among many is found to be one and the same, it is not the result of error, but of tradition."[18] Here again we see tradition, then still largely oral, used as an argument that a denomination had continued in the true Faith, in contrast to allegations that a later interpretation of scripture is superior to the traditional one or that a religious truth was lost in the first one or two centuries AD, and was "discovered" or "restored" in more recent times. Succession was a judge or safeguard of the correctness of hermeneutics, and not vice versa. His *Prescription against Heretics* regarded the doctrine transmitted by the apostolic succession as the criterion of doctrinal orthodoxy. To prove a church was in due succession, and therefore carried the true tradition, an inquirer was to consult its doctrine and the archival rolls of its bishops and its relation to other congregations. In contrast, Protestants generally believe that the faith and doctrine of the apostles and of apostolic men is found in the Bible, and can reconstructed from it

---

16. Tertullian, *Prescription against Heretics* 21.
17. Tertullian, *Prescription against Heretics* 20.
18. Tertullian, *Prescription against Heretics* 28 (ANF 3:256).

alone, often a laborious and complicated process, with results rejected by other Protestants. According to Tertullian, a person who wishes to obtain the fullness of the gospel need only unite him/herself with a local congregation founded by an apostle or a man ordained by an apostle or one whose doctrine agreed with theirs:

> But if there be any (heresies) which are bold enough to plant themselves in the midst of the apostolic age, that they may thereby seem to have been handed down by the apostles, because they existed in the time of the apostles, we can say: Let them produce the original records of their churches; let them unfold the roll of their bishops, running down in due succession from the beginning in such a manner that [that first bishop of theirs] bishop shall be able to show for his ordainer and predecessor some one of the apostles or of apostolic men,—a man, moreover, who continued stedfast with the apostles. For this is the manner in which the apostolic churches transmit their registers: as the church of Smyrna, which records that Polycarp was placed therein by John; as also the church of Rome, which makes Clement to have been ordained in like manner by Peter. In exactly the same way the other churches likewise exhibit (their several worthies), whom, as having been appointed to their episcopal places by apostles, they regard as transmitters of the apostolic seed. Let the heretics contrive something of the same kind. For after their blasphemy, what is there that is unlawful for them (to attempt)? But should they even effect the contrivance, they will not advance a step. For their very doctrine, after comparison with that of the apostles, will declare, by its own diversity and contrariety, that it had for its author neither an apostle nor an apostolic man; because, as the apostles would never have taught things which were self-contradictory, so the apostolic men would not have inculcated teaching different from the apostles, unless they who received their instruction from the apostles went and preached in a contrary manner. To this test, therefore will they be submitted for proof by those churches, who, although they derive not their founder from apostles or apostolic men (as being of

much later date, for they are in fact being founded daily),
yet, since they agree in the same faith, they are accounted
as not less apostolic because they are akin in doctrine.
Then let all the heresies, when challenged to these two
tests by our apostolic church, offer their proof of how
they deem themselves to be apostolic. But in truth they
neither are so, nor are they able to prove themselves to
be what they are not. Nor are they admitted to peaceful
relations and communion by such churches as are in any
way connected with apostles, inasmuch as they are in no
sense themselves apostolic because of their diversity as to
the mysteries of the faith.[19]

Tertullian here indicates that the apostolic succession at
Smyrna was just as important as that at the City of Rome for
purposes of deriving orthodoxy, by the apostolic succession and
particulars of doctrine.

Later, Tertullian converted from the mainstream church to
Montanism, and revised his views on apostolic succession accord-
ingly. In his earlier period, his view was similar to that of Irenaeus
that the apostolic tradition was transmitted through bishops and/
or presbyters,[20] but for Tertullian it was the congregations as cor-
porate bodies that were the guardians, with the bishops imparting
traditional teaching only as agents of the congregations, and the
succession-lists of bishops being merely the indicia that particular
churches were of apostolic origin or at least in comity with churches that had been founded personally by apostles or apostolic men.[21]
According to Tertullian, the later congregations received the fullness of the tradition from those of apostolic foundation by being
in communion with the earlier ones.[22]

---

19. Tertullian, *Prescription against Heretics* 32.1–8 (ANF 3:258).

20. Tertullian, *Prescription against Heretics* 20–21, 36 (between AD 198 and 202).

21. Tertullian, *Prescription against Heretics* 32; Tertullian, *Against Marcion* 1.21.

22. Tertullian, *Against Marcion* 4.5.

However, he had begun to identify the church and the Holy Spirit as a single entity.[23] This was significant in his later views. Under the influence of Montanism, Tertullian engaged in an elitism comparable to that of the Alexandrians Clement and Origen: the Spirit, the true church, was represented on earth by individuals of advanced spirituality and intellect, but "not the Church which consists of a number of bishops."[24]

Tertullian *On Modesty* 21:

> And accordingly "the Church," it is true, will forgive sins: but (it will be) the Church of the Spirit, by means of a spiritual man; not the Church which consists of a number of bishops. For the right and arbitrament is the Lord's, not the servant's; God's Himself, not the priest's.

Tertullian *Exhortation to Chastity* 7.5–7:

> It is the authority of the Church, and the honour which has acquired sanctity through the joint session of the Order, which has established the difference between the Order and the laity. Accordingly, where there is no joint session of the ecclesiastical Order, you offer, and baptize, and are priest, alone for yourself. But where three are, a church is, albeit they be laics. For each individual lives by his own faith, nor is there exception of persons with God; since it is not hearers of the law who are justified by the Lord, but doers, according to what the apostle withal says. Therefore, if you have the *right* of a priest in your own person, in cases of necessity, it behoves you to have likewise the *discipline* of a priest.

Note that any monopoly the bishop or other clergy possessed over administering the sacraments was instituted by the authority of the church rather than of God, which explains why it is not found in Scripture.

First Clement, Tertullian, and Irenaeus advocated apostolic succession only as the guarantor of correct doctrine and tranquility within the churches. They never said that the sacraments

23. Tertullian, *On Baptism* 6; *On Modesty* 21.

24. Tertullian, *On Modesty* 21 (ANF 4:100) (before AD 222).

and practical church administration of outside groups were invalid. Thus, a Christian can nevertheless be spiritually nourished and guided by discipline in an organization that does not claim a pedigree of bishops.[25] In fact, Tertullian noted that the sacraments can be administered by laity, and that the custom of restricting their performance to clergy is a human invention to promote sake of unity, peace, and good order within a church rather than a divine constraint:

> it remains to put you in mind also of the due observance of giving and receiving baptism. Of giving it, the chief priest (who is the bishop) has the right: in the next place, the presbyters and deacons, yet not without the bishop's authority, on account of the honour of the Church, which being preserved, peace is preserved. Beside these, even laymen have the right; for what is equally received can be equally given. Unless bishops, or priests, or deacons, be on the spot, *other* disciples are called *i.e. to the work*. The word of the Lord ought not to be hidden by any: in like manner, too, baptism, which is equally God's property, can be administered by all. But how much more is the rule of reverence and modesty incumbent on laymen—seeing that these *powers* belong to their superiors—lest they assume to themselves the *specific* function of the bishop! Emulation of the episcopal office is the mother of schisms.[26]

He also wrote at *On Baptism* 17 that laypeople are authorized to consecrate at a Eucharist.

G—Hippolytus *Apostolic Tradition*: AD 217

Although dated at AD 217, the *Apostolic Tradition* attributed to Hippolytus is generally regarded as describing the situation in central Italy a generation or two earlier. He had studied under Irenaeus. Long a presbyter in central Italy in early third century, he

---

25. See also: Second Vatican Council *Decree on Ecumenism* (*Unitatis redintegratio*) 3, November 21, 1964.

26. Tertullian, *On Baptism* 17.

became rival bishop of Rome from AD 217 to 235. He composed the book "in order that those who have been rightly instructed may hold fast to that tradition which has continued until now."[27] He assured his readers that "The Holy Ghost bestows the fulness of grace on those who believe rightly that they may know how those who are at the head of the Church should teach the tradition and maintain it in all things."[28] The book includes a role of the laity in the making of bishops: "He who is ordained as a bishop, being chosen by all the people" and "When his name is announced and approved, the people will gather on the Lord's day with the council of elders and the bishops who are present. 3 With the assent of all, the bishops will place their hands upon him, with the council of elders standing by, quietly."[29]

Among an ordained bishop's functions, the *Apostolic Tradition* includes the authority to bind and loose from sins,[30] offer gifts to God on behalf of the church, assign lots, and minister generally.[31] Presbyters are to govern the people[32] and share in the congregational council.[33] A deacon's powers are limited to "only what is confided in him under the bishop's authority."[34] A deacon is to be his bishop's errand boy.[35] Although the bishop is in charge of educating candidates for baptism and managing the arrangements,[36] it is a presbyter who baptizes[37] and anoints.[38]

---

27. Hippolytus, *Treatise on the Apostolic Tradition* 1.3, trans. Dix, 2.

28. Hippolytus, *Apostolic Tradition* 1.5, trans. Dix, 2.

29. Hippolytus, *Apostolic Tradition* 2.2–3 http://www.bombaxo.com/hippolytus.html.

30. Hippolytus, *Apostolic Tradition* 3.5.

31. Ibid.

32. Hippolytus, *Apostolic Tradition* 8.2.

33. Hippolytus, *Apostolic Tradition* 8.2–3.

34. Hippolytus, *Apostolic Tradition* 9.3–4.

35. Hippolytus, *Apostolic Tradition* 9.2–3.

36. Hippolytus, *Apostolic Tradition* 20.1–21.7, 22.1, 23.13–14.

37. Hippolytus, *Apostolic Tradition* 9.11.

38. Hippolytus, *Apostolic Tradition* 21.19.

Although the ordination ceremony (laying-on of hands) for a candidate which the people had elected to be bishop was always to be done by existing bishops, presumably of other congregations, a bishop would ordain his own presbyters and deacons without outside participation. This is the earliest known indication that ordination must be performed only by a bishop, not a deacon or presbyter, as officiating minister. In addition to the bishop, the incumbent presbyters lay hands or touch a candidate who is becoming a presbyter.[39]

Although the bishop was the officiating minister, the presbyters joined him in consecrating the bread and wine as the Eucharist.[40] Hippolytus regarded it as "presumptuous" or contrary to "discipline" for laypeople to consecrate the eucharistic elements.[41] This last, and a similar provision in Ignatius *Smyrnaeans* 8.1–2 (see below), is contradicted by Tertullian *On Baptism* 17. Instead of an outright prohibition, the *Apostolic Tradition* and Ignatius (see below) may mean merely "unlawful but valid."

---

39. Hippolytus, *Apostolic Tradition* 8.1.

40. Hippolytus, *Apostolic Tradition* 4.2.

41. Hippolytus, *Apostolic Tradition* 26.12.

4

Examining Older and Contemporary Sources for Apostolic Succession

THE PROBLEM WITH RELYING too much on *1 Clement*, Irenaeus, Tertullian and Hippolytus is that they all wrote from a western Mediterranean position, two or three coming to us through Western copyists, which may have been different from the much larger Christian realm in the East. For instance, monepiscopacy arrived in the west as the form of congregational government over half a century after its being instituted in the Middle East. To obtain a full view of the Christendom in which they wrote, we must (1) examine the full dimensions of *1 Clement* to ascertain which of the episcopal powers now claimed by advocates of apostolic succession were actually included in the Epistle, (2) consult writings earlier than Irenaeus and Tertullian to ascertain whether their views were products of the late second century and did not make their first appearance closer to the time of the apostles, and (3) determine whether there was positive or negative corroboration of their teachings elsewhere in the Christian world, such as the eastern Roman Empire.

A—Second Look at *1 Clement*

First Clement covers a large variety of related themes. It exhorts to obedience to God, love for other people, humbleness, peace, peace within the church, concord, unity within the church, orderliness, glorifying God, submission to presbyters, and self-sacrifice for the common good. It condemns sedition, envy, strife, disparagement of third parties, factionalism, schism, and party spirit within the church. It stresses amicable relations with other Christians more than obedience to existing authority. Despite the wide range of topics covered, it does not identify the powers, authority, responsibilities, or jurisdiction of elders and deacons nor declare whether the benefit conferred by the overthrown ones consisted of their leadership as governors, teachers of doctrine, authority to consecrate the Eucharist, or power to ordain either within the congregations or successors for other sees. *First Clement* does not touch on any inherent charism of clergy ordained in the apostolic succession, but only the duty to submit to them in undefined ways. Thus, the Epistle is of no assistance in ascertaining whether the specific powers or attributes can be transmitted only by an unbroken lineage of ordinations from the apostles, and what is the province of Christians generally, specifically laity.

First Clement also included a moral and behavioral requirement for retaining presbyters in the protected category: they must have "blamelessly served the flock of Christ in a humble, peaceable, and disinterested spirit, and have for a long time possessed the good opinion of all."[1] According to Irenaeus, the apostles were desirous that their appointees "should be very perfect and blameless in all things"[2] He also wrote that "those who possess that succession of the Church which is from the apostles, and among whom exists that which is sound and blameless in conduct, as well as that which is unadulterated and incorrupt in speech."[3] Such ideals did not last into the early third century. Shortly before the

---

1. *1 Clement* 44.3 (ANF 1:17).
2. Irenaeus, *Against Heresies* 3.3.1 (ANF 1:415).
3. Irenaeus, *Against Heresies* 4.26.5 (ANF 1:498).

Decian Persecution of AD 249–51, some presbyters and bishops used their power over appointments in the church to amass fortunes for themselves and their families instead of appointing on the basis of merit.[4] Many bishops and presbyters who presided over congregations sold many of them to "unsuitable persons" and ordained "undesirable men" to the Christian ministry,[5] many or all of whom were "greedy, tyrannical, and wicked."[6] Some clergy did not leave the selection of their successors to God but bequeathed their offices in their Wills to their relatives and thus established dynasties within the church.[7] The natural conclusion is that the beneficiaries were of similar or lesser character and fitness as their predecessors. To their credit, there are no extant accusations that any of them committed sexual sins. Here we find a beginning of the longstanding attitude of many clergy who regard their place in the apostolic succession as a private possession, immune from earthly intervention. Failure of medieval and later bishops to meet the moral qualifications, including sins of the flesh, would thus render doubtful their eligibility for ordination and/or protection from deposition from existing office.

The motive and message of 1 *Clement* were that the apostolic succession of presbyters and deacons should be preserved because only it could guarantee unity and co-operation and harmony in ministry. It opposed the unjustified exchange of elders and deacons within the congregational structure, but not the organizational polity of the Corinthians. There was another qualification,

4. Carl Vernon Harris, *Origen of Alexandria's Interpretation of the Teacher's Function)*, 217. Dr. Harris was professor emeritus of classical languages and literature, Wake Forest University. Harris' endnote (on p. 265) begins "Cf. *Hom. on Num.* XII.4", but, in Méhat's and Doutreleau's editions, 12.4 has no bearing on the subject matter. See instead Origen, *Homilies on Numbers* 9.1, 22.4.

5. Origen, *Commentary on Matthew* 16.22, trans. Arnold Ehrhardt *Apostolic Succession* 149. Arnold Ehrhardt was a German legal historian, church historian, and theologian.

6. Arnold Ehrhardt *Apostolic Succession*, 148, citing Origen but not identifying the work.

7. Origen *Homilies on Numbers* 22.4.1.

now overlooked, in order for a person to enter into the succession: to become a presbyter or deacon he must have been elected by the laity, with perhaps other clergy voting also: "with the consent of the whole Church."[8] I wonder whether Roman Catholic bishops in the twentieth and twenty-first centuries are qualified in that they are chosen directly and only by the pope.

B—The *Didache*: First Century AD

According to a Roman Catholic priest and author, "The oldest non-biblical document that we know is the anonymous *Didache*."[9] It is also the first church manual or directory of how to administer a church. It was written in Egypt or Syria in first century or early second century AD, and may predate the Gospel of Matthew.[10]

The *Didache* 15.1 instructs congregations to appoint their own presbyters and deacons, rather than ask an apostle or other bishops to do so, or even to confirm them in office. In the *Didache*, apostles are wanderers and possess no powers beyond what the individual congregations are willing to give them. Likewise, in Paul's epistles, there are both true and false peripatetic apostles (e.g. 2 Corinthians 11:13), who are not specially commissioned for church government. It might be argued that apostolic succession may have been instituted as a reaction to false apostles and to counteract them. However, the depiction of apostles as free-roaming teachers with uncertain authority persists in Revelation of John 2:2, which is conceded to be the last writing of any of the original Twelve. In the first three decades of the third century, *Didascalia* 23 and 25 also warn against false apostles, which indicates they were still current in that era.

To provide the benefits Irenaeus and Tertullian mentioned, we must narrow down the concept "succession from an apostle" to "succession from a true apostle." It would not be enough to say

8. *1 Clement* 44.3 (ANF 1:17).

9. Thomas M. Kocik, *Apostolic Succession*, 22 © the Society of St. Paul.

10. Aaron Milavec, *The Didache: Faith, Hope and Life*, passim. Professor of various Christian disciplines at various tertiary institutions.

a bishop's pedigree from an apostle protects his church(es) from heresy, for the first of his lineage may have been a heretic. Thus, a bishop claiming apostolic succession today must prove not only the concept, and his own place in the line, but also the specific member of the Twelve from which he descends. Despite his extensive church-planting, no lineage today claims Paul as its founder.[11] Apparently, some Christians appeared to have asserted that Paul was a false apostle, or not an apostle at all, judging by the many times he defended his status.[12]

In short, the earliest book of church instruction and administration contraindicates apostolic succession as conceived in our time.

C—Ignatius: about AD 107

Ignatius was a bishop of Antioch in Syria who had personally known the (true) apostles. During a persecution, the government took him into custody and sent him to the City of Rome to be executed. The route included the eastern shore of the Aegean Sea. On the journey he wrote letters to local churches and to Polycarp, a bishop of one of them who had also known the apostles. Although the main message of Ignatius's epistles was that Christians should respect and hold firmly to their clergy as appointees of God, he never alluded to apostolic succession as the grounds for it, or advocate what Irenaeus and Tertullian later wrote on at length.

Although Ignatius exhorts his readers to hold their bishops in high regard, and to be subject to them, he says the same about deacons and presbyters.[13] He even puts subjection "to one another" on the same level as that to the bishop.[14] One of his addressees was Polycarp, the bishop or leading presbyter of Smyrna in Anatolia, and may have been "the angel of the church in Smyrna" in Revelation

11. Ehrhardt, *Apostolic Succession*, 21, 67–68.

12. 1 Corinthians 9:1–2; 2 Corinthians 11:5, 12:11; Galatians 1:1; Galatians 2:8; 1 Thessalonians 2.6; 1 Timothy 2:7; Titus 1:1.

13. E.g. *Epistle to Ephesians* 2.2, 20.2; *Trallians* 13.2; *To Polycarp* 6.1.

14. Ignatius, *Magnesians* 13.2.

of John 2:8. He in turn began his own letter with "Polycarp and the presbyters with him" and asked the Philippian Christians to be subject to one another,[15] as well as to the presbyters and deacons.

Ignatius also alluded to the bishop's role in the liturgy and sacraments: "Let that be deemed a proper Eucharist, which is [administered] either by the bishop, or by one to whom he has entrusted it." Did Ignatius mean that consecration by anyone else was absolutely void or merely contrary to good order within the church? According to the same Roman Catholic priest, construing Ignatius's *Letter to the Smyrnaeans*, "But in Ignatius we do not find the terminological precision between "valid" and "licit" that is available/24/today; hence we cannot be certain if he intended to say that nothing happens sacramentally to the bread and wine used in unauthorized liturgies."[16]

The theme and purpose of all Ignatius' letters to congregations are to promote unity, including unity between clergy and laity and among the clerics themselves. According to early Christian literature and common experience today, members of the church without regard to office or status participate in a wide variety of church activities. For lay participation, everything is lawful in church matters but not everything is expedient (1 Cor 6:12, 10:23). Ignatius seems to be indicating that it is not expedient for unauthorized laity to consecrate the Eucharist but ought to subordinate their Christian liberties to avoid the schisms that would tend to result if they did not. Note that he did not limit the class of potential appointees to presbyters, but left it open for bishops to appoint laypeople to administer the sacrament as well.

Ignatius more probably seems to envision a practice like the "lay presidency." In some Lutheran denominations, the chief officer (sometimes called a "bishop") of a synod may appoint a layman to consecrate the bread and wine when it is unlikely that a pastor or other regularly-ordained minister will be in the locality for a

---

15. Polycarp, *To Philippians* 5.3.

16. Kocik, *Apostolic Succession*, 23–24.

long time. According to Wikipedia, lay presidency is the norm in the United Methodist Church.[17]

The following verse has attracted less attention from scholars: "It is not lawful without the bishop either to baptize or to celebrate a love-feast; but whatsoever he shall approve of, that is also pleasing to God, so that everything that is done may be secure and valid." Here Ignatius prohibits a practice "just to be on the safe side." Mainline churches today generally profess that anyone can validly baptize (valid), even a Jew or other non-Christian, even in circumstances where it would be contrary to the denomination's canon law (illicit). The Church of Rome long insisted in "conditional baptism" of converts previously baptized in other Christian churches because the intent might not be the same, but in recent years has entered agreements with most other families of denominations to recognize each other's baptisms; this is probably what Ignatius envisioned as whatever the bishops "shall approve of."

Ignatius's writings display an obsession with relationships among members within individual congregations, while silent on those between congregations. Despite his emphasis on respect for and obedience to clergy, he did not identify the powers, authority, responsibilities, or jurisdiction of elders and presbyters. Ignatius reveals nothing of the concept of apostolic succession or power over choosing or ordaining either within the congregations or successors for other sees. If there were, Ignatius would have been more than eager to include reference to it.

D—Polycrates AD 180s

In the days of Irenaeus, there was a major dispute in the church over the proper date for celebrating Easter and the authority to set the date. In a letter to the bishop of Rome in favor of the different tradition in his part of western Anatolia, Bishop Polycrates of Ephesus, speaking for the churches thereof, cited the large number of congregations in favor of their practice as an authority for it,

17. "Lay presidency."

and also the multitude of Christian leaders living and dead who agreed with it, including apostles, bishops, and Polycarp, and living "brethren throughout the world."[18] He thus indicated that the apostolic tradition was an authority but was silent about any apostolic succession, evidently showing that the latter was not accepted as a compelling argument by his group or that of Rome.

E—The *Didascalia*: First Three Decades of Third Century

According to internal evidence, when heresy or corruption entered the church on two occasions, the apostles intervened to set things right, with no mention of them appointing bishops or other clergy to guide and correct the churches on a permanent basis. Instead of a means of succession among officeholders, or method of choosing new ones, they left the *Didascalia* as a compendious written guide that supplied for any lack in coverage by the Scriptures. Somehow the bishops were to regulate matters, with no indication of their source of authority or indication of how to handle novel issues not covered in the Scriptures or the *Didascalia*.

The *Didascalia* holds a high view of every bishop, describes his powers, and advocates that laity render all submission and dependence to him. He possesses great, heavenly, almighty jurisdiction over body and soul, not least the authority to bind and loose from sins (Chapter 9). He sits and rules in the place of Almighty God (9). He is the normal officiant at baptism, the Eucharist, and preaching, and is an unchallengeable teacher of the Christian mysteries. He is always the chief justice in church courts in matters of sin and disputes between Christians (6 and 11). He controls sole jurisdiction to appoint presbyters, deacons, subdeacons, deaconesses, and assessors (9).

The bishop is to be the sole recipient of gifts to the congregation and its causes (9):

18. Letter to Victor at Eusebius *Ecclesiastical History* 5.24.1–7, especially v. 7.

> And thou shalt require no account of the bishop, nor ob-
> serve him, how he dispenses and discharges his steward-
> ship, or when he gives, or to whom, or where, or whether
> well or ill, or whether he gives fairly; for he has One who
> will require, even the Lord God, who delivered this stew-
> ardship into his hands and held him worthy of the priest-
> hood of so great an office. Wherefore, that thou observe
> not the bishop, nor require an account of him, nor speak
> ill of him and oppose God, nor offend the Lord.[19]

(This strikes me as more like the functions of the seven "deacons" in Acts.6.1–6.)

"Therefore love the bishop as a father, and fear him as a king,
and honour him as God." (9)

The *Didascalia* is against sedition, envy, strife, factionalism,
party spirit, and schism in church matters, especially in church
government. It encourages obeying God, obeying clergy (especially the bishop), humbleness, loving one another, peace, peace
within the church, concord, unity, glorifying God, submission to
presbyters and bishop, and self-sacrifice for the common good. It
commands the laity to pursue these under the leadership of the
bishop, who is under a special obligation to promote them and be
himself a model of them. Yet not a word as to how bishops receive
their authority and high office.

F—Early Churches Without Apostolic Succession

Because bishops were clearly vital church offices, great labors must
be exerted to ensure that only fit men attain the office, and some
warrant of their source of authority. Yet the *Didascalia* provides
absolutely no indication of how they were elected, appointed, or
ordained. The earlier church manual, the *Didache*, said election
by the laity. Contemporaneous with the *Didascalia*, Hippolytus's
Apostolic Tradition said election by the laity but an ordination ceremony by bishops from other churches.[20] Where we should expect

19. Connolly, 98,100.

20. *Apostolic Tradition* 1.1–3.

most to find a divinely-commissioned source of selecting bishops, there is no indication of any sort, which would indicate that its authors thought it not worth mentioning, or so well known as not to include in an otherwise voluminous and detailed church manual.

These might be dismissed as arguments from silence, and therefore weak. However, (1) as quoted above, Irenaeus made similar arguments from silence when asserting that the presbyters or bishops in succession neither knew nor taught the doctrines of the sectarians he was refuting, and (2) we do not find assertions of apostolic succession in the very places we would most expect to find them, written by ancient individuals who would gladly seize any opportunity to find support for the episcopacy for which they held the utmost regard. On the other hand, maybe some congregations or geographical regions were governed in accordance with apostolic succession while others possessed some other form(s) of church polity and selection; we are working here with scant evidence at a remove of nineteen centuries. In different countries and confessional nuances, Lutherans have for centuries employed a wide variety of polities and combinations of polities, with little or no criticism of the constitutional frameworks of other Lutheran groups. We already know that monepiscopacy was well developed and the norm in the East well before it spread to the City of Rome; if this be so, churches today can govern themselves equally with or without it, and with or without a lineage of succession from the apostles. For instance, Saint Jerome noted that for the church at Alexandria, from its founding by Mark the Evangelist until Dionysius the Great (the fourteenth bishop, died AD 264), the local presbyters always elected and ordained a bishop from their own number. Thus, even this strong Catholic church father around AD 400 saw the presence of other bishops to be unnecessary at the ordination of a new bishop of Alexandria,[21] with whom the entire Great Church was in communion.

21. *http://www.newadvent.org/fathers/3001146.htm St. Jerome's Letter CXLVI.* See also Kenneth J. Woollcombe, "Ministry and the Order," 48–50, 62, in Kenneth M. Carey (ed) "Appendix to the Second Edition." In *The Historic Episcopate*, 2d ed., 128–29. Woollcombe was a Fellow and Chaplain of St. John's College, Oxford.

A variety in church polity and ordination from region to region and time to time would indicate that they are of human invention rather than divine, and the local body of Christians can modify them as suits current circumstances, as a practice of their liberty in Christ.

5

The Bishops Themselves

5 A—Laying-on Hands not Sufficient

ACCORDING TO PROFESSOR PETER Stockmeier of the University of Munich, worship in the church described in the *Didache* required

> suitable superintendents, men who have taken the place the charismatic prophets and teachers, having attained this position by election. According to this instruction it is not appointment by existing office-bearers but the people's choice—made, admittedly, in accordance with specific criteria—which calls a man into the service of bishop and deacon. Hence the Didache proves that in Syria and Palestine of the second century election "from below" claimed a kind of equality with the endowment of the Spirit "from above."[1]

Around AD 240 Origen mentioned the requirement that the whole congregation be assembled for clerical ordinations, with the floor open to commendations and objections.[2] Origen (AD 185 to 254/255) was the foremost Christian theologian and teacher of the third century, and the most prolific Christian writer prior to Martin Luther, after the invention of printing with the birth of mass

---

1. Peter Stockmeier, "The Election of Bishops," 3–9 at 5.
2. Origen, *Homilies on Leviticus* 6.3.1.

media. Origen was a presbyter after AD 230. From AD 202 to 230 or 233 he was the dean/principal of the same institution of higher learning as Clement of Alexandria had been. In AD 231 or 233 he established his own at Caesarea in Palestine. Origen travelled much in the eastern Roman Empire as a theological consultant to local churches, at the requests of their bishops, and thus could observe Christian practice throughout the Middle East.

At least in Carthage and the City of Rome, the practice of election by the people survived into the years during and shortly after the thoroughgoing Decian Persecution and mass apostasy of AD 249–51. Bishop Cyprian of Carthage wrote approvingly of the result of a disputed election in the City:

> Cornelius was made bishop by the judgment of God and of His Christ, by the testimony of almost all the clergy, by the suffrage of the people who were then present, and by the assembly of ancient priests and good men, when no one had been made so before him, when the place of Fabian, that is, when the place of Peter and the degree of the sacerdotal throne was vacant.[3]

In the Epistle numbered 67 in both CSEL and ANF, Cyprian noted in AD 257 that candidates for clerical office are not to be ordained without the consent of the laity, "especially since they themselves have the power either of choosing worthy priests, or of rejecting unworthy ones." (v. 3) and:

> we observe to come from divine authority, that the priest should be chosen in the presence of the people under the eyes of all, and should be approved worthy and suitable by public judgment and testimony; as in the book of Numbers the Lord commanded Moses, saying, "Take Aaron thy brother, and Eleazar his son, and place them in the mount, in the presence of all the assembly, and strip Aaron of his garments, and put them upon Eleazar his son; and let Aaron die there, and be added to his people." God commands a priest to be appointed in the presence of all the assembly; that is, He instructs and shows that

3. Cyprian, CSEL *Epistula* 55.8; *Epistle.* 51.8 (ANF 5:329.

the ordination of priests ought not to be solemnized
except with the knowledge of the people standing near,
that in the presence of the people either the crimes of the
wicked may be disclosed, or the merits of the good may
be declared, and the ordination, which shall have been
examined by the suffrage and judgment of all, may be
just and legitimate.[4]

However, Cyprian wrote the following in a time of gradual de-
cline of the influence of the lower orders, a trend to give more and
more powers to the bishops (which reduced those of the laity), and
expanding the bishops' jurisdiction to include several congregations:

to the elders and deacons, and to the whole people, greet-
ing. In ordinations of the clergy, beloved brethren, we
usually consult you beforehand, and weigh the character
and deserts of individuals, with the general advice. But
human testimonies must not be waited for when the divine approval precedes.[5]

Some Roman Catholic scholars in our time agree that election was by the congregation rather than a supra-congregational
authority:

One of the fundamental laws of Christianity in the first
three centuries was that the local community, both "clergy and people," had the right to choose its own presidents
or leaders. That right was respected by popes and was
even confirmed by them, several times quite explicitly,
as inviolable. [6]

In the undivided Church of the first four centuries
the participation of the laity, where it occurred, was
considered an integral part of the spiritual event which

---

4. ANF 5:370 v. 4.

5. Cyprian, *Epistula* 32.1, or *Epistle* ANF 5:311–12. Same numbering in
CSEL.

6. Peter Huizing and Knut Walf, *Electing our own Bishops*, vii. Huizing is
a prolific writer on Roman Catholic topics, and is probably a Jesuit. Prof. Dr.
Walf is a German Roman Catholic theologian.

included election, ordination and reception of the newly ordained bishop.[7]

In these early centuries, the nominations and elections of bishops were done solely by a popular vote of all the faithful. St. Cyprian believed elections prevented unworthy persons from becoming bishops.[8]

Professor Stockmeier notes: "A survey of the history of official appointments in the early Church demonstrates that bishops were undoubtedly elected by clergy and people from the beginning."[9]

According to a professor emeritus of Fordham University,

> The current practice in the Latin Church of papal appointment of bishops, without any real input by either the clergy or the people of the diocese, is a comparatively recent development, first formally affirmed in the Code of Canon Law promulgated in 1917 (c. 329.2)[10]

Another Roman Catholic source indicates:

> Today most bishops in the Latin church are directly appointed by the pope, but that is a recent development. For most of the church's history, there was not a single way to select a bishop but a number of ways depending on the locale and the historical period.[11]

---

7. Edward J. Kilmartin, "Episcopal Election," 39. Kilmartin was a Jesuit and professor of theology at the University of Notre Dame, and has been published in the field of the ordained ministry.

8. Juicio Brennan, *An Intriguing History*. Juicio Brennan is software architect and professional theologian, Omaha.

9. Peter Stockmeier, "The Election of Bishops," 8.

10. Joseph F. O'Callaghan, *Electing our Bishops*, 5 © Rowman & Littlefield Publishers, Inc. He was Professor Emeritus of Medieval History, Fordham University.

11. John Huels and Richard R. Gaillardetz, *Selection of Bishops*. Prof. Huels was a North American Servite priest (Servites of Mary—OSM), former Provincial for the Eastern Province of the Servites in the USA (Chicago), and Full Professor of Canon Law at St. Paul's University in Ottawa, Ontario. He has been laicized since the time he wrote. Dr. Richard R. Gaillardetz is the Joseph Professor of Catholic Systematic Theology at Boston College and the current chair of the Boston College Theology department.

All these raise the question of whether the legitimacy and validity of a bishop depends in part on having been elected by his constituency, not just hands placed on him by pedigreed bishops of other localities. If so, the apostolic succession was broken for many sees.

B—The Entitlements and Responsibilities of Bishops

Ye therefore, who laid the foundation of this sedition, submit yourselves to the presbyters, and receive correction so as to repent, bending the knees of your hearts. Learn to be subject, laying aside the proud and arrogant self-confidence of your tongue.

—1 CLEMENT

As can be seen from the foregoing chapters, the laypeople's chief duties to their bishops were obedience and submission. But what are submission and obedience? How extensive are they? Were bishops to be the sole source of direction for the people under their care (like a dictator), or were there limits (as in a constitutional democracy)? There is a difference between limited authority (such as Queen Elizabeth) and absolute authority (like Edi Amin). What was the scope of Christian liberty while still showing the bishop submission and obedience? The earliest Christian authors envisaged limits and conditions on them, and allowed room for judgment and flexibility.

First Corinthians 16.16 commands submission, not only to local clergy, but to every fellow worker that helps and labors in the gospel. *First Clement* 38.1 mandates: "let everyone be subject to his neighbor." More widely, Ephesians 5.21 encourages "submitting yourselves to one another in the fear of God." First Peter 5.5 says not only "ye younger, submit yourselves unto the elder," but also "Yea, all of you be subject to one another." Besides submission to the bishop, Ignatius a generation later wished that it be rendered "to one another, as Jesus Christ to the Father, according to the flesh, and the apostles to Christ, and to the Father, and to the Spirit," as noted above. Nor can anything be more comprehensive than "Submit yourselves to every ordinance of man for the Lord's sake" (1 Peter 2.13).

Remember that Ignatius exhorted his readers to be subject not only to their bishops, but also their deacons and presbyters.[12] He put subjection "to one another" on the same level as that to the bishop.[13] "Polycarp and the presbyters with him" also asked the Philippians to be subject to one another,[14] as well as to the presbyters and deacons.

If everybody is subject to everyone else, especially other Christians, are not husbands in some way to submit to their wives? Does not such subjection reduce the rigor and degree of deference demanded when interpreting the New Testament and patristic passages just quoted?

Romans 13 contains the rule for church members not to oppose authority:

> 1Let every soul be subject unto the higher powers. For there is no power but of God: the powers that be are ordained of God. 2Whosoever therefore resisteth the power, resisteth the ordinance of God: and they that resist shall receive to themselves damnation. . . . 5Wherefore ye must needs be subject, not only for wrath, but also for conscience sake. 6For for this cause pay ye tribute also: for they are God's ministers, attending continually upon this very thing. 7Render therefore to all their dues: tribute to whom tribute is due; custom to whom custom; fear to whom fear; honour to whom honour.

Submission to the head of state "as supreme" is mandated in 1 Peter 2.13 "for the Lord's sake" while the following verse extends compliance "unto governors, as unto them that are sent by him for the punishment of evildoers." Elizabeth II is the head of state in

---

12. E.g. Ignatius, *Epistle to Ephesians* 2.2, 20.2; Ignatius, *Trallians* 13.2; Ignatius, *To Polycarp* 6.1.

13. Ignatius, *Magnesians* 13.2.

14. Polycarp, *To Philippians* 5.3.

most Commonwealth countries, but she possesses no power over life and death, nor even to tax without the consent of Parliament.

The above quotation from Romans may sound like absolute authoritarianism, but Acts 4:19–20 and 5:29 teach that we must obey God rather than men, thus indicating that there is an exemption from the rule, and thus hint that there may be other exceptions to commands to obey and submit. In Western democracies, obedience and submission do not prevent Christians, including Christian clergy, from signing petitions, complaining about politicians, voting against the party in power, or running for office themselves. All that is forbidden is violence and removing rulers by methods not specified in the country's constitution. The situation addressed in *1 Clement* was clearly a removal by unconstitutional means. "Sedition" is the name given to it in *1 Clement* and secular law.

Hippolytus indicates that the laity have the right and duty to intervene whenever incumbent clergy depart from the heritage of the apostles,[15] and, indeed, wrote *Apostolic Tradition* for them to deal with such a situation, such as a bishop who sinned a sin unto death,[16] a ground which *1 Clement* specifically stated was *not* the situation in the church at Corinth.[17]

Origen mentioned that some clergy were afraid of the laity,[18] which fear could exist only in an organizational arrangement with strong lay influence.

Remember Tertullian's statement that the transmission of authority in the postapostolic age was to groups rather than individuals. The bearers of correct doctrine were the local congregations with the bishop indicating its status, not a sole authoritative hierarchy set over one or more of them. From the frequent mention of presbyters in the ancient literature (always mentioned in the plural), it appears that a bishop was not the sole recognized trustee of the apostolic succession. Orthodoxy and justice were to be determined by the consensus of the many, rather than the fiat of the few.

15. Hippolytus, *Apostolic Tradition* Prologue 1.3–5.

16. Hippolytus, *Philosophumena*, or *Against Heresies* 9.7.

17. *1 Clement* 44.3–4.

18. Origen, *Homilies on Joshua* 7.6.

C—Episcopal Teaching Powers Were Not Exclusive

In *Stromata* 6.13 Clement of Alexandria refers to a tradition of correct doctrine, borne by individual Christians who devote themselves to the study and life inculcated by the Word, but who are not necessarily clergy. Clement mentions the threefold ministry of bishop, presbyter, and deacon only to parallel "the angelic hierarchy."[19]

In the Preface to *De Principiis*[20] Origen laid great and repeated emphasis on the proposition that the true teaching was imparted to "the church." At Preface 2–3 and 4.14 he agreed with Clement that there is sufficient scope within the tradition for a gifted individual to find scriptural truths that are concealed from less scholarly or less perceptive Christians. At 4.9 Origen wrote that the apostles handed down the standards they had received in a succession from Christ to the "teachers" of the church. Remember that Irenaeus did not specify the office or title of the person in "the most ancient Churches with which the apostles held constant intercourse" as the solver of disputes if the Scriptures had not been complete.[21] According to a variant and disputed scholium of his commentary on Luke 10:30–36, Origen regarded both bishops and teachers (*didaskaloi*) to be the successors of the apostles as ministers of the church and as guardians of the tradition. [22] In keeping with reliance on scholars who might not be clergy, Origen proposed in his *Commentary on the Gospel of Matthew* that whenever a question arises on a point of the Christian religion, the disputants should "go to any of those who have been appointed by God as teachers in the church."[23] To Origen, the guardians of orthodoxy were "the teachers," not "the bishops," although he does not deny that through study a bishop may be also a scholar and therefore a

19. Kocik, *Apostolic Succession*, 32.

20. Especially *De Principiis* Preface 2.

21. Irenaeus, *Against Heresies* 3.4.1.

22. Origen, Fragment 71 of "Les fragments grec" of *Homélies sur s. Luc*, 520–521.

23. Origen, *Commentary on Matthew* 13.15 (ANF 10:413).

teacher. Indeed, Origen had no specific word for "preacher" but called himself simply a *didaskalos* or teacher, a kind of educator.[24]

Such teachers held an ancient office in Christianity, older than that of presbyters (including bishops) and deacons. The usual title of Christ in the four Gospels is "teacher," especially in the synoptics.[25] In the twenty-seven-book New Testament, Jesus is referred to as "bishop" only in 1 Peter 2:25 and nowhere as "presbyter" or "elder." In 1 Corinthians 12:28, Paul places teachers below only apostles and prophets as God's appointees in the operation of the church, while he ranks governors/administrators as seventh or next to last, who were bishops and presbyters or the predecessors of bishops and presbyters. Second Peter 2:1 to 22 is a lengthy warning against false teachers in the church, which could well indicate that Christians of the time were acquainted with the office of an orthodox teacher. Second Timothy 4:3 is to the same effect. A collection of purported divine revelations in the early or mid-second century, the *Shepherd of Hermas* spoke of apostles, bishops, deacons, and teachers as distinct ministries.[26] It is prophets and teachers that *Hermas* mentioned as preaching Jesus.[27] *Didache* 13.2 spoke of teachers as synonymous with prophets. When Christianity was first introduced to a locality it was by apostles, prophets, or teachers preaching the word, winning converts and nurturing them in the faith; bishops/presbyters and deacons did not make an appearance until after the labors of an apostle, prophet, or teacher resulted in establishing a Christian congregation there.[28] Origen

24. Joseph T. Lienhard, "Introduction" to *Origen: Homilies on Luke*, xx.

25. Matthew 8:19; 9:11; 12:38; 17:24; 19:16; 21:15; 22:16; 22:24; 22:36; 26:18; Mark 4:38; 5:35; 9:17; 9:38; 10:17; 10:20; 10:35; 12:14; 12:19; 12:32; 13:1; 14:14; Luke 3:12; 7:40; 8:49; 9:38; 10:25; 11:45; 12:13; 18:18; 19:39; 20:21; 20:28; 20:39; 21:7; 22:11; John 1:38; 8:4; 11:28; 20:16.

26. *Hermas* Vision 3.5.1.

27. *Hermas* Similitude 9.15.4.

28. 1 Corinthians 16:15–16; Origen, *Homilies on Numbers* 11.4.5; Arnold Ehrhardt, *Apostolic Succession*, 96; Richard Patrick Crossland Hanson, *Origen's Doctrine of Tradition*, 181. Hanson was Professor of Historical and Contemporary Theology, University of Manchester; Anglican clergyman and educator in Ireland and England, Bishop of Clogher, 1970–73.

opined that a local church could be founded by "someone,"[29] without specifying that he or she must already hold one of these offices.

For over two centuries of early Christianity, the offices in 1 Corinthians 12:28 were not mutually exclusive: it was not as if a person were unable to hold only one of the eight offices at a time. Both Paul and Barnabas were teachers as well as prophets and apostles (Acts 13:1). According to the Pastoral Epistles, most or all bishops/presbyters were also teachers (1 Tim 3:2; 4:11; 4:13; 5:17; 2 Tim 2:24; 4:2; Tit 2:1). Ephesians 4:11 links teachers with pastors as a function in the church distinct from those of apostles, prophets and preachers. *Didache* 15.1 speaks of bishops and deacons as performing the ministry of teachers and prophets, although the following verse appears to indicate that the latter two held a distinct ministry. It was not until the era during and after the Decian Persecution as a time of departure from the original patterns of Christianity that the teaching office became exclusively monopolized by bishops and presbyters.[30] The offices of apostle, teacher, and prophet disappeared by this point.[31] Irenaeus of Lyons did not make a distinction between the teacher as competition to the clergy of bishops, presbyters, and deacons because he combined the offices of teacher and cleric in his own person.[32]

This reinforces the conclusion that bishops' powers in the mainstream/catholic church were not all-encompassing, even in the third century.

---

29. Origen, *Homilies on Numbers* 11.4.5, trans. Thomas P. Scheck, 56.

30. Joseph T. Lienhard, "Introduction" to *Origen: Homilies on Luke*, xx. Fr. Lienhard is a Jesuit and professor at various Roman Catholic institutions of higher learning.

31. Arnold Ehrhardt, *Apostolic Succession*, 84.

32. Arnold Ehrhardt, *Apostolic Succession*, 138. For more on the office of *didaskaloi*, see E. Prinzivalli, "Didaskalos" in *Encyclopedia of the Early Church* (New York: Oxford University Press, 1992), 1:235; G. L. Prestige *Fathers and Heretics* (London: S.P.C.K., 1940; repr. 1954), 25–26, 44–45. Fellow and Chaplain of New College, Oxford, Secretary of the Church of England Council for Foreign Relations; Carl Vernon Harris, *Origen of Alexandria's Interpretation of the Teacher's Function in the Early Christian Hierarchy and Community*.

6

Old Testament as a Model

THERE IS A NEW argument in support of the current claims for apostolic succession and episcopal or papal exclusivity. It is based on the idea that the institutions of the Old Covenant are models for what should be applied in the New. It runs that "a church with apostolic succession flows more naturally out of the Old Testament narrative." Just as God established a priesthood in a hierarchy that began with Aaron and continued in a line of succession until the time of Christ, so God established a new priesthood over Christians with all the rights and powers of the Levitical priesthood. This establishing was part of Christ fulfilling the Law and continuing the divine will. Christians are therefore to depend for the forgiveness of sins and correct religious teaching on Christian (meaning Roman Catholic) priests, with succession from the apostles being substituted for the Aaronic line. Because Levitical priests did not lose their status despite their sinfulness, so the sinfulness of Catholic clergy does not disqualify them from office or break the line of succession, nor relieve the child of God of their obligation to worship only through priests. A visible hierarchy in a succession is necessary in order for the Bible to be correctly interpreted.[1] As for the argument of some Protestants that there can be no distinct clerical office among Christians because we constitute

1. *Convinced to be Catholic*, Apostolic Succession Part 2.

a "priesthood of all believers," proponents for this model point out that the whole Israelite nation were also priests (Exod 19:6), yet God established a special visible hierarchical priesthood from among one of their tribes.

The first flaw in this hypothesis is that the succession of Aaronic priests was and remains easily identifiable. The succession was biological and hereditary, confined to the sons of earlier priests. No layman could ever become a Levitical priest. In times of disruption or long interruption of divine worship, new clergy could be identified because succession was in family lineages. Even today, a Jew knows whether he is descended from and a member of the priests (cohen), the Levitical assistants (Levi), or a layman (Yisroel), through father telling son throughout the millennia as to which segment of the Hebrew population they belong. This will be important if the long-lasting hope of some Jews is fulfilled that they can restore the sacrificial system after retaking Temple Mount. By contrast, most Christian clergy come from the general population, regardless their biological ancestry; there is no natural or obvious means of finding men (and in some cases women) to fit into the number. In fact, Roman Catholicism precludes a man from inheriting priesthood from his father, because celibacy is mandatory in the Latin Rite. Ordination and promotion within an episcopal hierarchy is uncertain, unlike the Old Testament system, and has left wide doubts (e.g. Hippolytus and the Avignon schism) as to who really is the bishop. In contrast to the maneuvering and careerism among Roman Catholic bishops, there was no way a Jewish priest could raise or lose status.

Secondly, the Aaronic priests were ceremonial priests and nothing more, someone who offered ritual sacrifices. They were not teachers or exegetes of the Law. In Christ's time, this was performed by the scribes, who claimed to pass down the oral tradition and correct interpretation from the time of Moses. New moral instructions and divine messages came through the prophets, who were often at odds with the priests and sometimes criticized them. Although they occasionally exercised judicial powers, the priests did not dominate secular rule, which was left to the kings, elders, and chiefs of tribes, except for the Maccabean period. By the time of Jesus, they were a mere partisan minority, not the governing party, and were obliged to share control of the Sanhedrin with the Pharisees, a lay movement.

As disclosed in the New Testament and other early Christian literature, Christian clergy included teachers, administrators, exegetes, and rulers. Officiating eucharistic sacrifices was only occasional in comparison to their other functions. Except for Christ and the whole people of God as a priesthood of all believers, neither the New Testament[2] nor Greek fathers before the third century[3] called any Christian office-bearer a "priest" (*hiereus*), except that *Didache* 13.3 mentions the wandering prophets to be a congregation's "high priests," and this may be only an analogy. Until the third century AD, Christian clerics were not likened to Aaronic and Levitical ones, or even called "priests," but servant, elder, or overseer (deacon, presbyter, or bishop in Greek), and perhaps teacher. This term and the idea of priestly sacrifices within Christianity, were thus late in coming, long after Irenaeus.

2. *Shorter Lexicon of the Greek New Testament by F. Wilbur Gingrich, rev. by Frederick W. Danker* (Chicago: University of Chicago Press, 1983); George Ricker Berry *The Interlinear Literal Translation of the Greek New Testament* (Grand Rapids, Michigan: Zondervan, 1958); *New Testament Greek Lexicon King James Version*, based on Thayer's and Smith's *Bible Dictionary*, plus others. It is keyed to the large Kittel and the *Theological Dictionary of the New Testament* https://www.biblestudytools.com/lexicons/greek/kjv. Entries *Archiereus* and *Hiereus*.

3. Geoffrey William Hugo Lampe, *A Patristic Greek Lexicon* (Oxford: Clarendon Press, 1961) 238–39, 669–70. https://archive.org/details/LampePatristicLexicon. Professor, theologian, and Church of England priest who dedicated his life to theological teaching and research.

7

The Purpose of Apostolic Succession

SECOND TIMOTHY 2.2 INSTRUCTS "And the things that thou hast heard of me among many witnesses, the same commit thou to faithful men, who shall be able to teach others also." The verse does not specify elders or bishops. It relates to doctrine, not sacraments or church discipline.

The motive and message of *1 Clement* were that the apostolic succession of presbyters and deacons should be preserved because only it could guarantee unity and co-operation and harmony in ministry under men of good character who had proved themselves both before and after they were ordained. It does not include other matters claimed for bishops in episcopal denominations today.

Tertullian and Irenaeus advocated apostolic succession only as the guarantor of correct doctrine. They never said that the sacraments and practical church administration of outside groups were invalid. Thus, a Christian can still be spiritually nourished and guided by discipline in an organization that does not claim a pedigree of bishops.[1]

Irenaeus was concerned chiefly with doctrine. He cited the succession only in addition to the widespread acceptance of a form of the *Apostles Creed* throughout the Mediterranean and barbarian

---

1. Tertullian, *Exhortation to Chastity* 7.5. See also: Second Vatican Council, *Decree on Ecumenism* (*Unitatis redintegratio*) 3, November 21, 1964.

lands. For him, unity was based and manifested in a universal creed handed down by tradition, rather than a universal hierarchy. He gave its contents four times in *Against Heresies* 1.10.1, 1.22.1, 3.4.2, and 5.20.1, and once in *Demonstration of the Apostolic Teaching* 6. The fact that he stated it five times reveals he was referring to a phenomenon well accepted by all Christians of his day and it was fairly uniform. He proffered this as universally observed, not limited to one city or geographic region.

In *Prescription against Heretics* 32 Tertullian is less concerned about who teaches the doctrine in the church than about the content of the teaching itself. Chapter 20.5–9 of the same book considered the apostolic tradition of truth to be transmitted by congregations themselves, not necessarily by bishops. For him, ecclesial legitimacy and doctrinal orthodoxy of a congregation derive not from recognition or certification by a central or even regional authority of the universal church, but through having been founded by an apostle or being founded in turn by one of these congregations, or founded in a line of foundations from such congregations ("offspring"). What was important to him was the content of the tradition rather than its bearer.[2] A congregation which was not founded directly by the apostles may nevertheless be apostolic if its interpretation of the Scriptures and other doctrinal teaching is the same as congregations which had.

---

2. Kocik, *Apostolic Succession*, 28.

8

Apostolic Succession did Not Work

EVEN SINCE CHRISTIAN ANTIQUITY, apostolic succession has failed to guarantee unity of doctrine and co-operation and harmony in ministry. In the third century itself, contending factions split the church at Rome, first involving Hippolytus and later Novatian, both claiming with much credibility that they were descended from apostolic pedigrees. Better known is the Avignon or Western Schism from 1378 to 1417, during which different countries in western Europe recognized different men as sole vicar of Christ. There were also the repeated ejections and restorations of bishops/patriarchs of Constantinople. The famous Athanasius of Alexandria went through five such cycles.

The Wikipedia article "Old Catholic Church"[1] details a vast variety of denominations and fellowships with apostolic succession through the laying-on of hands by bishops in the Roman lineage, but now divided by a multitude of differences on ethics, dogma, and practice. Some denominations claiming apostolic succession for their clergy deny that particular other denominations possess it although these others assert the same claim and inherit similar lineages. Even while the present book was being written, Anglicans were flying every which way over a variety of issues, while still recognizing the pedigrees of their opponents, with Free

1. "Old Catholic Church."

Church of England, Reformed Episcopal Church, Orthodox Angli-
can Church, Anglican Catholic Church, Anglican Church of Vir-
ginia, Anglican Orthodox Church, Anglican Orthodox Southern
Episcopal Church, Anglican Church in America, Anglican Province of America, Anglican Province of Christ the King, Christian
Episcopal Church of North America, Diocese of the Holy Cross,
Episcopal Missionary Church, Holy Catholic Church (Anglican
Rite), Orthodox Anglican Church, Anglican Catholic Church of
Canada, and United Episcopal Church of North America, to name
a few. Some of these divisions touch on theology or administration, which means Hegesippus, Clement, Irenaeus, and Tertullian
would be disappointed with institutional succession in office, and
find another way of preserving orthodoxy, order, and unity. Any
principle of apostolic tradition has been discredited most by the
people who claim it for themselves.

In establishing apostolicity, Hegesippus listed only a few
pedigrees of bishops. We would expect a roll of successions for
prominent sees such as Ephesus and the other six churches which
are known to exist from the Revelation of John.

The roll of bishops for which we possess the best attestation is
the City of Rome. Yet, there is much doubt as to who the first successors of Peter were. Around AD 180 Irenaeus wrote that Peter and
Paul instituted Linus as the first Roman bishop and then Anacletus,
Clement, Evaristus, and Alexander followed.[2] However, Tertullian
around AD 200 offers an incompatible account. Instead of Peter and
Paul instituting Linus as the first Roman bishop and then Clement being third in the list as Irenaeus claimed, Tertullian said Peter
ordained Clement as the first Roman bishop. Clement went from
being the third bishop of Rome to the first.[3] Tertullian wrote:

> For this is the manner in which the apostolic churches
> transmit their registers: as the church of Smyrna, which
> records that Polycarp was placed therein by John; as also

---

2. Irenaeus, *Against Heresies*, 3.3.3.

3. Ibid.
Tertullian, *Prescription against Heretics* 32.

the church of Rome, which makes Clement to have been ordained in like manner by Peter.[4]

A Calvinist commentator of our own time observes:

> There are contradictory late second century and early third century succession lists of alleged Roman bishops. Why is this so? Many scholars note it is because there actually was no succession of a single bishop until A.D. 150. This is why such later church fathers contradicted each other on who the earliest single bishop was.[5]

It is odd that there was a contradiction in the succession-list of reputedly the most important and most-watched church officer in Christendom. The discrepancy cannot have been because no one early enough had made a list, with Tertullian relying on distant memory. About the time of Bishop Anicetus (AD 155 to 166), Hegesippus compiled a succession-list for the City,[6] which was known to Eusebius but has since been lost. This may be as expected, because Hegesippus's search was for orthodox doctrine among the several churches, rather than legitimate church government or sacramental validity through a line of ordinations from the apostles.[7] Hegesippus drafted lists of bishops of some other localities, and concluded that Christianity had everywhere remained doctrinally pristine until the second or third bishop after the apostles, with the dividing line around AD 100. Thus, he believed in apostolic succession but also that it had lost its value over eighteen centuries ago. These lists also are not extant. Whatever continuity Rome possessed was broken in the Hippolytus-Callistus or Cornelius-Novatian schisms, or those concerning Avignon in the Middle Ages, with two or sometimes three men claiming to be bishop of Rome, and even a fourth. Still less did Irenaeus or Tertullian foresee a single city being the headquarters of Roman

4. Ibid.

5. Keith Thompson, "Later Contradictory Succession Lists of Roman Bishops." Mr. Thompson affirms the 1689 *London Baptist Confession of Faith*.

6. Eusebius, *Ecclesiastical History* 4.22.3.

7. Eusebius, *Ecclesiastical History* 4.22.1–4.

Catholic, Eastern Orthodox, Eastern Catholics of more than one rite, Episcopal/Anglican, and uncounted other bishops in the apostolic succession, as is the case in North America and Australia today. As originally conceived, the theory of apostolic succession just does not provide for these situations.

Eusebius of Caesarea was the first major church historian. He painstakingly surveyed the whole church in the Roman Empire and quoted material from other writers which are otherwise lost. In his *Chronicle* and *Ecclesiastical History*, written in the AD 320s, Eusebius displayed a diligence and aptitude for historical and archival research, giving information on kings of all manner of obscure city-states and larger political entities. Yet he recorded the bishops of only four sees, even though he adverts to some individual bishops of other places in passing. For Rome, he was dependent upon Irenaeus, and *Ecclesiastical History* 5.6 does not list bishops beyond those in *Against Heresies*, nearly a century and a half earlier. Irenaeus himself regarded it as "very tedious" rather than important to list more than a single local pedigree.[8]

Whether the lineages of local bishops were not kept up to date or not preserved because the pagan government destroyed them or because Christians regarded succession itself as no longer of consequence, the fact remains that they have been lost and there is no way to trace with the all-important continuity to our times that its advocates posit.

After the legalization of Christianity in Eusebius's time, and continuing to the twenty-first century, the doctrine of apostolic succession has come to operate on the dangerous assumption that questioning the wisdom of persons who currently hold authority is ecclesiastical treason, and secular treason as well in the Middle Ages. Modern practitioners of apostolic succession often extend it into areas of teaching and action far beyond what the ancients contemplated. The theory has come to encroach on the rights of other clergy and laity, and given bishops a jurisdiction not contemplated by the earliest literature.

---

8. Irenaeus, *Against Heresies* 3.3.2 (ANF 1:415).

9

Apostolic Succession Cannot be Proved

WHILE THE IDENTITIES OF bishops in a pedigree were ascertainable when Irenaeus and Tertullian wrote, later generations would know them only as names on a long list and be unable to verify if the list was accurate. As in the above case at Rome, sometimes there was more than one list, for rival claimants. Sometimes there were and are more than one claimant to the same bishopric, such as that of Antioch, with no way through bishops-rolls to choose among rivals. Today there are five claimants, representing the Syriac Orthodox Church, the Greek Orthodox Church of Antioch, the Syriac Catholic Church, the Melkite Greek Catholic Church, and the Maronite Church. There was also a Latin Rite Patriarch of Antioch, until 1964. All claim succession through the notorious Paul of Samosata, whom church councils had a Roman Emperor depose for gross corruption and heresy. [1]

Despite bandying about the succession at Smyrna as a classic example and proof of universal succession, the records proffered by Irenaeus, Tertullian, and Eusebius contain only the first two names.

All sees claiming apostolic foundation today assert that they were founded by one or more of the original Twelve or by men whom the New Testament records as having been in close

---

1. "Patriarch of Antioch."

association with them, including Paul and Barnabas.[2] However, they cannot exhibit valid rolls of their predecessors. Exceptions are Aquileia,[3] Alexandria, and Philip the Evangelist for Ethiopia,[4] but there are gaps of over two hundred years between the first Christian contact and the establishing of a local church organization as we know it, such that we are tempted to dismiss ancient foundations as legends. The same is true of the Russian Orthodox Church, claiming descent from Andrew the Apostle.[5] As in other localities, apostolic succession is claimed on the sole basis of an apostle having preached there, without founding a permanent Christian community or leaving probative evidence of a bishop or continuity of Christianity of any sort. Similar claims by congregations, dioceses, and whole denominations can also be dismissed as wishful thinking, unless they can affirmatively prove a list of bishops rooted in apostolic times.

There are about five thousand Roman Catholics in our day who claim to be bishops in a line of ordinations from the apostles. Some 96½ % of them trace their pedigree no further back than an Italian bishop who was appointed in 1541. There is no documentary evidence as to who ordained him.[6] Thus, almost no present Roman claim can be verified as far back as can the Protestant churches with an episcopal polity. For instance, Swedish Lutheran bishops can trace their pedigrees from 1531, a decade earlier, and before that supposedly through Roman Catholic lines,[7] because a Roman Catholic bishop appointed by the pope of Rome ordained him. It is unknowable whether either lineage descends from a false apostle.

2. "Sees or Churches viewed as founded by apostles.'"

3. "List of bishops and patriarchs of Aquileia."

4. "Origins." In "Ethiopian Orthodox Tewahedo Church."

5. "Russian Orthodox Church."

6. Charles N. Bransom Jr., *Apostolic Succession in the Roman Catholic Church.* Bransom has researched and written on apostolic succession and episcopal lineages for over forty-five years. He is editor and publisher of the *Revue des Ordinations Épiscopales.*

7. "Laurentius Petri."

For the status of the succession in my home area, I contacted the Anglican diocese, asking if it possesses a roll going back from its present incumbent to the apostles, and asked whether I could come and look at it. In response to my third attempt, the archivist ended her email with "We have no such list" and an expression of regret that she could not help me in this matter.[8]

I also wrote to the local Roman Catholic archdiocese. The reply contained an impressive number of ordinations, going back to the Renaissance. Three early predecessors to the present Archbishop were in three different lineages, with the earlier two claiming only as far back as fifteenth-century popes,[9] and the latest (present) starting with the aforesaid Italian bishop appointed in 1541. There was a seven-year break in the 1870s in Nova Scotia, something like the two-year-long vacancies after four popes in the Middle Ages.[10] This is in sharp contrast to Irenaeus and Tertullian, who contemplated consulting the bishop-rolls to be a quick and easy process.

I invite readers of the present book to make similar inquiries from the archives of their local dioceses.

If the succession of bishops is indispensable to the life of the church, then the gates of hell must have prevailed against it during these periods. This is not the case if the essential is a worshipping community, even if composed wholly of laypeople.[11] The same doubts are true of the patriarchs of Antioch. If gaps can be ignored, with the Holy Spirit and divine authority jumping over them, then the principle applies to sects descended from Herbert W. Armstrong which assert open proof in their succession until the early third century and allege it persisted in secret until public ordinations

---

8. Lorraine Slopek, email to author February 27, 2019. Slopek is Diocesan Archivist, Diocese of Nova Scotia and Prince Edward Island, Anglican Church of Canada.

9. Sharon E. Riel, email to author January 28, 2019. She works for the Archives, Archdiocese of Halifax-Yarmouth, Nova Scotia, Roman Catholic Church.

10. "List of extended *sede vacante* periods."

11. Matthew 18:18–20; Tertullian, *Exhortation to Chastity* 7.5.

recommenced in the twentieth century.[12] If long breaks in lineage over worshipping communities be of no consequence, Latter-day Saints can rely on their contention that the Christian church disappeared around AD 100 and was fully restored in the 1830s, with full apostolic power. Actually, ancient Christians rejected the possibility of such a scenario when they disallowed the Montanists' contention that the Holy Spirit somehow escaped the apostles and first descended on Montanist prophets in the middle of the second century, replacing the mainstream church.

For that matter, there is always a break in the succession in denominations where the bishops serve life terms, and the successor is not elected or appointed until after the incumbent's death, e.g. bishopric of Rome, papacy. The situation is otherwise where a bishop serves for a predetermined term of years, and does not give up their functions until after their successor is chosen, e.g. archbishop of Canterbury. In the former case, there is a delay—a gap in continuity—until the appointer or electoral college can decide on a successor, while in the latter the retiring bishop often helps to install his successor. An unbroken lineage is more consistent with the latter, but is the exception among non-Protestants. The first-century literature would seem to favor ordination before rather than after death, because the first bishops were installed in office during the lifetimes of the apostles, who went on their separate ways to ordain and otherwise serve elsewhere. The early fathers after *1 Clement* are silent on the point, except for Origen's mention of some clergy trying to appoint their successors in their Wills, but next he mentions rowdiness at meetings of lay electors, with like disapproval.[13]

The lineages of bishops may be included in the "genealogies" warned against in 1 Timothy 1:4 and Titus 3:9. Today's advocates of apostolic succession appear to fit what Irenaeus described as "certain men have set the truth aside, and bring in lying words and vain genealogies, which, as the apostle says, 'minister questions rather than godly edifying which is in faith.'" [14] In the AD 180s,

---

12. Bob Thiel, "Claims of Apostolic Succession."

13. Origen *Homilies on Numbers* 22.4.1.

14. Irenaeus, *Against Heresies* 1 Preface 1.

he wrote that anyone could ascertain "the succession of these men to our own times;"[15] the present problem is tracing it since then.

Apostolic succession seemed like a good idea when first proposed, but so did Prohibition, community of goods, the Russian Revolution of 1917, and many marriages. Subsequent practitioners have learned better and formed different evaluations.

15. Irenaeus, *Against Heresies* 3.3.1.

10

———

The Onus of Proof

A SELF-EVIDENT MAXIM OF secular law is that "he who asserts must prove." It is not enough to flatly state that early Christians were regulated by apostolic succession. Because it is usually impossible to prove a negative, the onus is on the proponents of the applicability of such succession today to prove their argument from ancient sources. In *Prescription against Heretics* 32 Tertullian placed the onus of proof on claimants, to be discharged by showing bishop-rolls and correct doctrine. A third reason for thus placing the onus is that the denominations of its proponents demand that members reorient their lives, submit to the denomination's teaching in every regard, and donate money to it throughout their lives. To be a Roman Catholic, you must live each day in the fear that your diocesan bishop may close down your local worshipping community and oblige you to travel far further to attend the compulsory weekly Mass. A convert to Orthodoxy (both Eastern and Oriental) must forsake their identity and their ancestors in order to fit into their exclusively ethnic churches. Becoming an Anglican is like moving to a country at civil war. The consequences of accepting a theory of succession, and which line of succession, must also be weighed in the process of evaluating the evidence for it.

In Christianity, too many people allege that an apostolic or other early state of affairs had existed, without substantiation from original contemporary or near-contemporary sources. As far as I have been able to ascertain, proponents of the succession make only a bald statement that it is so as if it were established and indisputable fact, without offering lists for more than four or five bishoprics, all of them before AD 325, and even some of these may be drawn from late fabrications created for the purpose, rather from records contemporaneous with the listed bishops.

All teaching and practice must be affirmatively proved from the best evidence available. Otherwise, any sort of statement can be made about anything, and that which can prove anything proves nothing. It is the same as the allegations of some Protestant sects urging inquirers to join them because "the Bible says" that early Christians worshipped on Saturday instead of Sunday or held a belief or combination of beliefs found at the present day only in the denomination that is making the claim. Ask them to point out the Bible book and verse that say this. The burden is similarly on the proponents of the theory of succession to show us the lists of bishops in lineage, as Irenaeus and Tertullian did and exhorted other Christians to do. To be persuasive, the succession-rolls must have been compiled within living memory of the persons they mention; too many are forgeries in whole or in part from later centuries. Here the onus of proof changes place because it is easier to prove a forgery than a lack of forgery.

11

The Alternatives

IRENAEUS CONSIDERED THE APOSTOLIC succession, and the apostolic tradition for that matter, as of value only if the New Testament were not available. This was at a time when the New Testament canon had not yet been settled:

Against Heresies 3.1.1:

> We have learned from none others the plan of our salvation, than from those through whom the Gospel has come down to us, which they did at one time proclaim in public, and, at a later period, by the will of God, handed down to us in the Scriptures, to be the ground and pillar of our faith.[1]

Against Heresies 3.4.1:

> how should it be if the apostles themselves had not left us writings? Would it not be necessary, [in that case,] to follow the course of the tradition which they handed down to those to whom they did commit the Churches?[2]

Against Heresies 4.33.8:

---

1. ANF 1:414.
2. ANF 1:417.

True knowledge is [that which consists in] the doctrine of the apostles, and the ancient constitution of the Church throughout all the world, and the distinctive manifestation of the body of Christ according to the successions of the bishops, by which they have handed down that Church which exists in every place, and has come even unto us, being guarded and preserved without any forging of Scriptures, by a very complete system of doctrine, and neither receiving addition nor [suffering] curtailment [in the truths which she believes]; and [it consists in] reading [the word of God] without falsification, and a lawful and diligent exposition in harmony with the Scriptures, both without danger and without blasphemy; and [above all, it consists in] the pre-eminent gift of love, which is more precious than knowledge, more glorious than prophecy, and which excels all the other gifts [of God].[3]

Unlike the ancients, we today possess the apostolic teaching in conveniently-available New Testaments, which are commonly obtainable in inexpensive translations, or even free-of-charge from various Bible societies. This is in far contrast to ancient Christian times, when every book had to be copied by hand and was very expensive, most Christians living their entire lives without seeing a complete New Testament. This may account for why the doctrine of "Scripture alone" arose and became widespread shortly after the invention of printing. Reliance on clergy alone was the only method of proceeding before the advent of mass literacy in the nineteenth century and widespread university attendance since the 1960s. The extant documents of the apostolic tradition are also readily accessible, if a person is prepared to do enough reading of the remaining early sources that have been published in the original or in translation. All but one of them is available in English or French, and many on the internet, and some as audio recordings. A project is already underway to publish a translation of what I believe to be the last remaining one.[4] Given developments in tech-

---

3. ANF 1:508.

4. John B. Martino, email to author January 29, 2019, re: Origen's *Homilies on Psalms*. He is Acquisitions Editor at Catholic University of America Press.

nology since the invention of the printing press, we are in a better position to know the whole counsel of God than were Christians at the time of the formulation of the theory of apostolic succession and its reassertion in the sixteenth century.

Granted, there are many different interpretations of the Bible, usually from translations, about 30,000. Tertullian exhorted joining oneself with the denomination whose doctrine coincided with the teaching of the apostles. The only general rule that can be drawn is to avoid denominations that advance anything obviously and demonstrably contrary to the New Testament. Rejection of a denomination or its distinctives should not be based on just anything that is debatable or can be raised by an argument founded only on logic or modern-day anecdote, or require stitching a single verse in one part of the Bible to another and another, or analogy with horses or farming. Divisive interpretations should not be entertained in matters to which the New Testament gives little or no space. We must employ some other means to narrow down the remaining ones if we believe there is only one true church on the face of the earth. Because there is much agreement among the remaining denominations, there may today be more than one true church. The division among them is nowhere as great as between the heresies and the Great Church in Irenaeus's and Tertullian's time; for instance, all Christian denominations today agree that there is only one God, which was not the case of Marcion and the Gnostics.[5] There is also general consensus on which books comprise the New Testament today, which was absent in Christian antiquity.

We today can use the early post-biblical sources (including Irenaeus and Tertullian) as a lens or narrowing through which to interpret the Scriptures because they provide the best procurable evidence of how the first heirs of the Christ and the apostles understood their teachings, and as "a testimony and declaration of the faith, as to how at any time the Holy Scriptures have been understood and explained in the articles in controversy in the Church of God by those then living, and how the opposite dogma

5. Tertullian, *Against Marcion* 1.21.

was rejected and condemned."[6] Theirs is only a collection of opinions or perceptions or hearsay, but it is more probable than those of someone fifteen or twenty centuries removed from the milieu which surrounded its origin.

According to Tertullian, "in all cases of various practice, of doubt, and of uncertainty," the disputants ought to inquire as to "which of two so diverse customs were the more compatible with the discipline of God."[7] Whatever the common knowledge of Christian "discipline" among believers in early times, it survives with certainty today only in Scripture and apostolic tradition as described by other early Christian sources, or Scripture interpreted with the aid of them. The resort is therefore to the Bible now that there is substantial doubt as to whether anyone today is able to prove they are in the succession advocated by Tertullian and Irenaeus.

Irenaeus said that interpretation of Scripture and Christian belief should be guided by the creed, whose contents he set out five times.[8] Tertullian presented it in *Prescription against Heretics* 13. Hippolytus records that in AD 217 it was standard for baptisms, with the addition of belief in "the Holy Church and the resurrection of the flesh."[9] To us, it appears the same or very similar to the *Apostles Creed*. To narrow down the number of acceptable Bible interpretations and discern the full meaning of Bible texts, we should interpret it through the apostolic tradition preserved in this creed, and perhaps also through the *Nicene Creed* as evidence to what the whole church agreed on. Too often, small sects, which usually reject tradition and creeds, construe Scripture texts in the most contrary manner; interpretation in harmony with the creed(s) would produce more consistent and credible results, and fewer of them.

I am aware of the argument that we would not know which books are in the Bible had it not been for the decisions of various post-Nicene church synods, which Roman Catholics claim as

6. *Epitome of the Formula of Concord* Rule and Norm 8.

7. Tertullian, *Veiling of Virgins* 2.

8. Irenaeus, *Against Heresies* 1.10.1, 1.22.1, 3.4.2, 5.20.1; Irenaeus, *Demonstration of the Apostolic Preaching*, 6.

9. Hippolytus, *Apostolic Tradition* 21.17.

their own even though there was no separation from the Eastern Orthodox until centuries afterwards. Moreover, proponents of the argument extend it by alleging that because the bishops at the synods determined the extent of scripture, only their successors can interpret it, and if we accept the decisions of the councils as to contents, we are obliged to accept the totality of the claims to authority of them and of people who say they are their successors. This is too simplistic. The parameters of the canon were disputed for a long time before and after, and varied from region to region. Individual ancient writers produced canon-lists of their own, which varied from author to author and region to region. There was so little consensus on the issue within the catholic/Great Church that shortly after AD 396 the great Augustine felt it necessary to formulate a four-step method by which his readers could determine for themselves which books were canonical, a method which included consulting even other catholic churches overseas.[10] The "canonization" process was more like compiling dictionaries: a word does not become a word because it is in a dictionary, with the compiler free to put in or leave out at his/her discretion. The editors do not invent words, but merely report what words are in use in the language. The compilers are clerks scanning current practices in vocabulary, and arrive at a decision to include a word only on the basis of a wide spectrum of literary works. In the same way, the council fathers reported what most Christians regarded as Scripture, relying on the use among believers. Like dictionary editors, they did not authorize something new, but merely recorded what was already the prevailing practice. Because dictionaries are in plain language, there is no need for specially-qualified interpreters; what interpreters there may be look within the bounds of the dictionary itself, rather than contacting the compilers. Once the dictionary is published, the editors retain no authority over its use. In the same way, the synods did not retain power over how their canon was to be used. By publishing, compilers and council fathers relinquish all control over subsequent use of their labors.

10. Augustine, *On Christian Doctrine* 2.8.12.

Appendix

A REFERENCE TO AN early Christian writer may look impressive, and more so a quotation from one. But how do you know whether the writer of the present book—or any other author on the subject—copied the original sources correctly and did not take ancient material out of context? The present booklet provides information about all sources cited above, either in the first footnote about an author, or in the text itself. Then the following tells you how you can access the sources for yourself:

Except where otherwise indicated in the footnotes, all translations from church fathers before AD 325 are from *The Ante-Nicene Fathers; Translations of The Writings of the Fathers down to A.D. 325*. American reprint edition. Abbreviated "ANF." To access by author, then writing, google "ante nicene fathers" and select from the many sites displayed. My own favorite is http://www. biblestudytools.com/history/early-church-fathers/ante-nicene/, because it is machine readable, and enables quick access to any specific passage without knowing the page number in a print edition of a translation or the original. It provides much quicker and easier access from a quotation than does a paper text.

References to and quotations from Eusebius's *Ecclesiastical History* are from *Church History of Eusebius*. Translated by Arthur Cushman McGiffert. *Nicene and Post-Nicene Fathers Second Series* (NPNF 2d).

Translations of Eusebius *Ecclesiastical History* and many other ancient patristic works can be accessed on the internet. Some works before the end of the second century can also be accessed as audio recordings there, and more will probably be added during the time the present book is in circulation.

Translations of the church fathers published by the Catholic University of America Press are still in copyright, and thus do not appear free on the internet. Nevertheless, try googling anyway, in case new translations are posted during the years the present book is in circulation. The problem with translations published by CUAP and under some other Roman Catholic auspices is that they render the Greek word for "elder" (*presbuteros*) as "priest" for a Christian clergyman, even though the particular person held no sacrificial functions or powers now unique to clergy in episcopally-organized denominations. My way to ascertain the original Greek or Latin word is by consulting the book in the *Sources chrétiennes* series, published in Paris by Éditions du Cerf, which has French and the original language on facing pages.

Parts of Origen's commentaries on Matthew are under copyright, other parts are not. The ANF contains Books 10 through 14 and fragment of Book 2 in the *Philocalia* of the original Greek, no longer in copyright. They are also translated in *The Commentary of Origen on the Gospel of St Matthew* trans. Ronald E. Heine (Oxford, UK: Oxford University Press, copyrighted 2018), which also contains the *vetus interpretatio* of the Latin of Books 12 through 17, and the *Commentariorum Series*, from another Latin translation.

R. Hugh Connolly's *Didascalia apostolorum; The Syriac Version Translated and Accompanied by the Verona Latin Fragments* is available at http://www.earlychristianwritings.com/text/didascalia.html, where it is easier to study than the print edition (Oxford: Clarendon, 1929).

There are two common hardcover English translations of the *Apostolic Tradition* attributed to Hippolytus of Rome. One is *The Apostolic Tradition of Hippolytus* translated by Burton Scott Easton (New York: Macmillan; Cambridge, England: University Press, 1934). It is available in print and on the internet. The other is *The Treatise on the Apostolic Tradition of St Hippolytus of Rome*, edited by Gregory Dix; reissued with corrections by Henry Chadwick

Appendix

(London: Alban Press; Ridgefield CT: Morehouse, 1992). Having
been produced after 1923, it is still under copyright. However, if you
google for "Hippolytus Apostolic Tradition" through "bombaxo,"
you will find a third translation, which can be freely copied if you
credit bombaxo as the source. Note that the numbering of chapters
and headings differ from translator to translator; except where otherwise indicated, the present book uses that of Dix and Chadwick.

Joseph F. O'Callaghan, Thomas M. Kocik, and the essays in
Electing Our own Bishops, edited by Peter Huizing and Knut Walf,
can be accessed only in hard copy. Seminary and university librar-
ies are usually generous in issuing borrower privileges to members
of the general public. They sometimes charge an annual fee for
them. Unless you reside in a major metropolis or in a college town,
you will probably not find any of the items at a library locally. If
the book you want is not available at your public library, ask it for
what is called an "interlibrary loan," and show the attendant the
items in this book you wish to borrow. Your public library will
then obtain the book(s) for you. The library that owns the book
might or might not ask for a small fee. Check ahead at the public
library; the service might well be free of charge in your locality.
Provide as much information as possible regarding the title you
want, and give the information to the employees at the local public
library. Their staff will then research where the book can be bor-
rowed from and obtain it for you.

Bibliography

"Apostolic see." Accessed December 11, 2019. https://en.wikipedia.org/wiki/Apostolic_see.

"Apostolic succession." Accessed December 13, 2019. https://en.wikipedia.org/wiki/Apostolic_succession.

Arnobius. *Against the Heathen*. In ANF 6:413–540.

Augustine of Hippo. *On Christian Doctrine*. In *Nicene and Post-Nicene Fathers* First Series 1:519–97. Buffalo: Christian Literature Publishing, 1887.

Bramsom, Charles N., Jr. *Apostolic Succession in the Roman Catholic Church*. Accessed December 13, 2019. https://web.archive.org/web/20140924082501/http://mysite.verizon.net/res7gdmc/aposccs/.

Brennan, Juicio. *An Intriguing History: Election of Bishops in the Catholic Church*. Accessed December 13, 2019. *juiciobrennan.com/files/bishopselection/bishopSelectionFlier.pdf* © 2008.

Clement of Alexandria. *Stromata, or Miscellanies*. In ANF 2:299–567.

Connolly, R. Hugh. *Didascalia apostolorum; The Syriac Version Translated and Accompanied by the Verona Latin Fragments*. Oxford: Clarendon, 1929. http://www.earlychristianwritings.com/text/didascalia.html.

"Convinced to be Catholic, Apostolic Succession Part 2." Accessed January 1, 2020. https://www.youtube.com/watch?v=64IBYKKYCqk.

Cyprian. *Epistulae*, or *Letters*. In ANF 5:267–409.

Didache. In ANF 7:377–82.

Ehrhardt, Arnold. *The Apostolic Succession in the First Two Centuries of the Church*. London; Lutterworth, 1953; reprinted Eugene, OR: Wipf and Stock, 2009.

Epitome of the Formula of Concord (AD 1577). In *Triglot Concordia: The Symbolical Books of the Evangelical Lutheran Church*. St. Louis: Concordia Publishing House, 1921. http://bookofconcord.org/fc-ep.php.

Firmilian. *Against the Letter of Stephen*, or *Letter 75*. In the collection of Cyprian, ANF 5:390–397 (as Epistle LXXIV).

First Epistle of Clement. In ANF 1:[5]–21, ANF 10:[229]–48.

Hanson, Richard Patrick Crossland. *Origen's Doctrine of Tradition*. London: SPCK, 1954.

Bibliography

Harris, Carl Vernon. *Origen of Alexandria's Interpretation of the Teacher's Function in the Early Christian Hierarchy and Community*. New York: American Press, 1966.

Hippolytus. *Apostolic Tradition*. http://www.bombaxo.com/hippolytus.html.

———. *Philosophumena*, or *Against Heresies*. In ANF 5:9–153.

———. *The Treatise on the Apostolic Tradition*. Translated by Gregory Dix, reissued Henry Chadwick. London: SPCK, 1968.

Huels, John, and Richard R. Gaillardetz. *The Selection of Bishops: Exploring Canonical Alternatives*. https://richardgaillardetz.files.wordpress.com/2014/04/election_of_bishops.pdf.

Huizing, Peter, and Knut Walf. *Electing our own Bishops*, edited by Peter Huizing and Knut Walf; English language editor Marcus Lefébure. New York: Seabury Press; Edinburgh: T. & T. Clark, 1980. Copyright 1980, by Stichting Concilium, T. & T. Clark Ltd., and The Seabury Press Inc.

Ignatius of Antioch. *Letter to Polycarp*. In ANF 1:93–96.

———. *Letter to the Ephesians*. In ANF 1:49–58.

———. *Letter to the Magnesians*. In ANF 1:59–65.

———. *Letter to the Smyrnaeans*. In ANF 1:86–92.

———. *Letter to the Trallians*. In ANF 1:66–72.

Irenaeus of Lyons. *Against Heresies*. In ANF 1:315–567.

———. *Demonstration of the Apostolic Preaching*, translated by Joseph P. Smith under title *Proof of the Apostolic Preaching*. New York: Newman, 1952.

———. *Letter to Florinus*. In Eusebius *History of the Church* 5.20.4, translated by Arthur Cushman McGiffert NPNF 2d 1:238.

———. *Letter to Victor*. In Eusebius *History of the Church* 5.24.1–8, translated by Arthur Cushman McGiffert NPNF 2d 1:243–44.

Jerome. *Letter 146*. http://www.newadvent.org/fathers/3001146.htm St. Jerome's Letter CXLVI.

Justin Martyr. *Dialogue with Trypho*. In ANF 1:194–270.

Kilmartin, Edward J. "Episcopal Election: The Right of the Laity." In *Electing our own Bishops*, edited by Peter Huizing and Knut Walf, 39–43

Kocik, Thomas M. *Apostolic Succession in an Ecumenical Context*. New York: Alba House, c1996. © the Society of St. Paul

"Laurentius Petri." Accessed December 10, 2019. https://en.wikipedia.org/wiki/Laurentius_Petri.

"Lay presidency." Accessed January 25, 2020. https://en.wikipedia.org/wiki/Lay_presidency.

Lienhard, Joseph T. "Introduction." In *Origen: Homilies on Luke; Fragments on Luke*, xv–xxxix. Washington, D.C.: Catholic University of America Press, 1996.

"List of bishops and patriarchs of Aquileia." Accessed December 11. 2019. https://en.wikipedia.org/wiki/List_of_bishops_and_patriarchs_of_Aquileia.

Martyrdom of Marian and James. In Herbert Musurillo, *The Acts of the Christian Martyrs*, 194–213. Oxford: Clarendon, 1972.

Bibliography

Martyrdom of Pionius. In Herbert Musurillo, *The Acts of the Christian Martyrs*, 136–67. Oxford: Clarendon, 1972.

Milavec, Aaron. *The Didache: Faith, Hope and Life of the Earliest Christian Communities, 50–70 C.E.* New York; Mahwah, NJ: Newman Press, 2003.

O'Callaghan, Joseph F. *Electing our Bishops: How the Catholic Church Should Choose its Leaders.* Lanham, Maryland: Rowman & Littlefield, 2007.

"Old Catholic Church." Accessed December 10, 2019. https://en.wikipedia.org/wiki/Old_Catholic_Church.

Origen. *Against Celsus.* In ANF 4:395–669.

———. *Commentary on Matthew.* Books 1 and 2 [fragment], 10–14: In ANF 10:413–512.

———. *Commentary on the Song of Songs.* In *Origen: The Song of Songs: Commentary and Homilies,* translated and annotated by R. P. Lawson, 21–263. New York: Newman, 1957.

———. "Fragments grecs." In *Homélies sur s. Luc,* edited and translated by Henri Crouzel, François Fournier and Pierre Périchon, [464]–547. Paris: Cerf, 1962.

———. *Homilies on Exodus.* In *Origen: Homilies on Genesis and Exodus,* translated by Ronald E. Heine, 227–387. Washington, DC: Catholic University of America Press, 1982.

———. *Homilies on Isaiah.* In *Isaïe: Origène, Homélies traduites par Jacques Millet, Sermons d'Augustin, d'Eusèbe le Gallican, de saint Bernard, de Rupert de Deutz traduits par Jacqueline Legée et les Carmélites de Mazille,* 21–87. n.p.: Desclée de Brower, 1983.

———. *Homilies on Joshua.* Edited by Cynthia White. Translated by Barbara J. Bruce. Washington, DC: Catholic University of America Press, 2002.

———. *Homilies on Leviticus,* translated by Gary Wayne Barkley. Washington, DC: Catholic University of America Press, 1990.

———. *Homilies on Luke; Fragments on Luke,* translated by Joseph T. Lienhard. Washington, DC: Catholic University of America Press, 1996.

———. *Homilies on Numbers,* translated by Thomas P. Scheck, edited by Christopher A. Hall. Downers Grove, IL: IVP Academic, 2009.

———. *On First Principles, or De principiis.* In ANF 4:239–382.

"Origins." In "Ethiopian Orthodox Tewahedo Church." Accessed December 11, 2019. https://en.wikipedia.org/wiki/Ethiopian_Orthodox_Tewahedo_Church#Origins.

"Patriarch of Antioch." Accessed December 10, 2019. https://en.wikipedia.org/wiki/Patriarch_of_Antioch.

Polycarp. *Letter to Philippians.* In ANF 1:33–36.

Polycrates. In *Letter to Victor,* at Eusebius *History of the Church* 5.24.1–8, translated by Arthur Cushman McGiffert NPNF 2d 1:242.

Quadratus. *Apology.* In ANF 8:749.

Roberts, Alexander, and James Donaldson. *The Ante-Nicene Fathers: Translations of the Writings of the Fathers Down to A.D. 325.* Buffalo, NY: Christian Literature, 1885–96.

Bibliography

"Russian Orthodox Church." Accessed December 11, 2019. https://en.wikipedia.org/wiki/Russian_Orthodox_Church.

Second Vatican Council. *Decree on Ecumenism* (*Unitatis redintegratio*). November 21, 1964.

"*Sede vacante.*" "List of extended sede vacante periods in the Holy See from earliest times." Accessed December 11, 2019. https://en.wikipedia.org/wiki/Sede_vacante.

Stockmeier, Peter. "The Election of Bishops by Clergy and People in the Early Church." In *Electing our own Bishops*, edited by Peter Huizing and Knut Walf; English language editor Marcus Lefébure, 3–9. New York: Seabury Press; Edinburgh: T. & T. Clark, 1980.

Tertullian. *Against Marcion*. In ANF 3:[271]–474.

———. *De praescriptione haereticorum*, or *The Prescription against Heretics*. In ANF 3:243–65.

———. *On Baptism*. In ANF 3:[669]–679.

———. *On Modesty*. In ANF 4:74–101.

———. *On the Veiling of Virgins*. In ANF 4:27–37.

———. *Soul's Testimony*. In ANF 3:[175]–179.

———. *To Scapula*. In ANF 3:[105]–108.

Theophilus of Antioch. *To Autolycus*. In ANF 2:89–121.

Thiel, Bob. "Claims of Apostolic Succession", Continuing Church of God. Accessed January 1, 2020. https://www.youtube.com/watch?v=BHmlVQn_Pz8.

Thompson, Keith. "Later Contradictory Succession Lists of Roman Bishops." In "Absence of Papal Views Among the Earliest Christians" *Exegetical Apologetics* http://www.exegeticalapologetics.com/2018/05/absence-of-papal-views-among-earliest.html. Accessed December 11, 2019.

Williams, Daniel H. *Retrieving the Tradition and Renewing Evangelicalism: A Primer for Suspicious Protestants*. Grand Rapids, MI; Cambridge, UK: Eerdmans, 1999.

Woollcombe, Kenneth J. "The Ministry and the Order of the Church in the Works of the Fathers" In Kenneth M. Carey (ed). *The Historic Episcopate the Fullness of the Church: Six Essays by Priests of the Church of England*. 2d ed., 41–62. Westminster [England]: Dacre Press, 1960.

www.ingramcontent.com/pod-product-compliance
Lightning Source LLC
LaVergne TN
LVHW021615080426
835510LV00019B/2591